Idea
Mapping

How to
Access Your Hidden Brain Power,
Learn Faster, Remember More,
and Achieve Success in Business

Jamie Nast

WILEY

John Wiley & Sons, Inc.

Published by John Wiley & Sons, Inc., Hoboken, New Jersey.
Published simultaneously in Canada.

For general information on our other products and services please contact our Customer Care Department within the U.S. at (800) 762-2974, outside the U.S. at (317) 572-3993, or fax (317) 572-4002.

Wiley also publishes its books in a variety of electronic formats. Some content that appears in print may not be available in electronic books. For more information about Wiley products, visit our website at www.wiley.com

Library of Congress Cataloging-in-Publication Data:

Nast, Jamie, 1960–
   Idea mapping : how to access your hidden brain power, learn faster, remember more, and achieve success in business / Jamie Nast.
      p.   cm.
   Includes index.
   ISBN-13: 978-0-471-78862-1 (cloth/cd-rom)
   ISBN-10: 0-471-78862-7 (cloth/cd-rom)
   1. Creative ability in business. 2. Creative thinking. 3. Cognitive maps (psychology). I. Title.
   HD53.N37   2006
   650.1—dc22

                                                                            2006008030

Printed in the United States of America.

10 9 8 7 6 5

Contents

List of Figures   *iv*
Acknowledgments   *vii*
About the Author   *x*
Foreword   *xiii*
Preface   ,   *xvii*

Introduction   1
1 Battle of the Brains   5
2 What is an Idea Map?   19
3 Reading and Creating Idea Maps   35
4 The Three Basics of Idea Mapping   49
5 Detours   61
6 Applications   83
7 The Question of Software   121
8 It's a Process   149
9 Team Mapping Method   181
10 Breaking All the Rules   195
11 Your Presentation Revisited   223
12 Idea-Mapping Menu   229
13 Real-Time Idea Mapping—The Final Challenge   247
Appendix 1: Summary of Lessons   255
Appendix 2: More Information   257

Index   *259*
About the CD-ROM   *265*

List of Figures

Figure #	Caption Title	Page	Contributor
1.1	Covey Day-One Map	10	Jamie Nast
1.2	Chapter 1 Summary	16	Jamie Nast
2.1	The Tree of Knowledge	22	www.futureknowledge.biz
2.2	The Tree of the Philosophy of Love	23	www.futureknowledge.biz
2.3	Bloom of Ideas	29	Jamie Nast
2.4	Flow of Ideas	29	Jamie Nast
2.5	Bloom + Flow of Ideas	31	Jamie Nast
2.6	Chapter 2 Summary	34	Jamie Nast
3.1	The Laws of Idea Mapping	38	Jamie Nast
3.2	Idea Map Part I	44	Jamie Nast
3.3	Idea Map Part II	45	Jamie Nast
3.4	Idea Map Part III	46	Jamie Nast
3.5	Chapter 3 Summary	48	Jamie Nast
4.1	Identifying Main Branches	55	Jamie Nast
4.2	Drawing Simple Icons	57	Jamie Nast
4.3	Chapter 4 Summary	60	Jamie Nast
5.1	Key Words I	65	Jamie Nast
5.2	Key Words II	65	Jamie Nast
5.3	Alternate Solutions	67	Jamie Nast
5.4	Wrong	69	Jamie Nast

List of Figures

Figure #	Caption Title	Page	Contributor
5.5	Right	70	Jamie Nast
5.6	Wrong	71	Jamie Nast
5.7	Right	72	Jamie Nast
5.8	Chapter 5 Summary	81	Jamie Nast
6.1	Data Collection for Annual Job Review	87	Jared Kelner
6.2	Estate Planning	90	Liza Seiner
6.3	Decision	93	Vanda North
6.4	Vision	96	Jamie Nast
6.5	Vision—Getting Started	98	Jamie Nast
6.6	Problem Employee	101	Jamie Nast
6.7	Marketing Campaign	103	Jeff Alexander
6.8	Get Ahead	106	Pete Wilkins
6.9	Dual Core	108	Gregg Stokes
6.10	Cancer Map	110	Judy Bess
6.11	An Introduction to Leadership Coaching	114	Kirsty Hayes
6.12	Company Mission Statement	116	Gan F. Tong
6.13	Chapter 6 Summary	119	Jamie Nast
7.1	Cat Food Positioning Considerations	129	Terry Moore
7.2	Training/Learning Event	132	Vanda North
7.3	Cold Call	135	Andrei Jablokow
7.4	Initial Call	136	Andrei Jablokow
7.5	IT Project	138	Andrei Jablokow
7.6	Simulator Project	140	M. Kumar
7.7	Fiscal Year 2005 Summary	142	Pete Wilkins
7.8	Chief Knowledge Officer (CKO)	144	Trygve Duryea
7.9	Chapter 7 Summary	148	Jamie Nast

LIST OF FIGURES

Figure #	Caption Title	Page	Contributor
8.1	Chemical Warfare	154	Beth Schultz
8.2	Antihistamines	156	Beth Schultz
8.3	Antianemia Drugs	158	Beth Schultz
8.4	Antihypertensives	160	Beth Schultz
8.5	Antianginals	161	Beth Schultz
8.6	Uses of Idea Mapping	164	Debbie Showler
8.7	Introduction Presentation	165	Debbie Showler
8.8	To Do Map	167	Debbie Showler
8.9	One to One Map	168	Debbie Showler
8.10	Corporate Vision	170	Debbie Showler
8.11	Chapter 8 Summary	180	Jamie Nast
9.1	Chapter 9 Summary	194	Jamie Nast
10.1	EPA Regulation Summary	198	Michael Torpey
10.2	Orbiting the Giant Hairball	202	Megan Clark
10.3	Article Summary	204	Sandy Dietrich
10.4	Landmark	206	Choo Boo Lim
10.5	Before Photo	214	Michael Shaw
10.6	Current Photo	214	Michael Shaw
10.7	The Future	215	Michael Shaw
10.8	World Trade Center Memorial Park	219	Kaizad Irani
10.9	Chapter 10 Summary	221	Jamie Nast
11.1	Chapter 11 Summary	227	Jamie Nast
12.1	Chapter 12 Summary	246	Jamie Nast
13.1	Chapter 13 Summary	254	Jamie Nast

Acknowledgments

In my line of work, there is a great emphasis on the magnificence of the brain and its unlimited capabilities. It's my belief that our brains are a marvelous creation, and many times, what's been created often becomes the object of our wonder. Little credit, awe, or admiration finds its way to the Creator. So first and foremost I want to acknowledge God as Creator of the brain. He has given me all gifts, talents, and opportunities to teach and to share this book with you. My job is to be a good steward of this task and all His blessings.

The creation of this book is nothing short of a miracle. Both the proposal and the manuscript were written during the busiest season of work I have ever had. I needed to provide video footage of myself teaching a class to accompany the original book proposal. While under an extremely tight deadline, I left one of two videotapes I still needed to edit in a video camera in Vancouver, British Columbia. During the eventual editing of that video, our new 32-inch television fell off of the table where I had it hooked up to the video camera. It put a hole in our hardwood floor, broke the table, and scarred the television. While teaching in Palm Beach, Florida, during hurricane Wilma, I lost all of my publishing documents when the windows in my hotel room shattered and the wind sucked out everything that wasn't tied down. I was supposed to do some writing during those 2 weeks, but had no documents and no power. My season of writing continued like this clear through to the end, so my gratitude for its completion and everyone's support is beyond my grasp.

There are so many people to thank. It all started with Randy Raines who introduced me to a tool called mind mapping (which became the foundation of idea mapping) in 1991 and then instructed my first *Mind Matters* workshop in February of 1992. Vanda North, the founder and director of The Learning Consortium and previously the founder and global director of The Buzan Centres, certified me as a licensed instructor and has mentored and coached me since 1992. She also made some great suggestions for this book. I treasure her friendship and support. Tracey Berry and Suzanne Brown manage the office of The Learning Consortium in England, and they are my lifeline when it comes to organizing public workshops. The more than 14,900 individuals who have attended my workshops have shaped the experiences that I now share with you. I've also had the privilege of certifying a global network of instructors. They are like family to me.

A big "thank you" goes to Heather O'Connor for calling me and asking me to write this book. Scott Hagwood introduced me to Jodie Rhodes who is an extraordinary literary agent. Angelo Lam and Catherine Ho provided the infamous video footage that finally made its way from Vancouver; and Patty Sophiea edited the final video that went into the proposal package for Wiley. And of course there is the team at Wiley—especially Matt Holt, Shannon Vargo, Kate Lindsay, Christine Kim, and Deborah Schindlar. Thank you for your patience as we worked together through this project.

This book would not be possible without all of those who contributed their idea maps and stories. I am so grateful for their willingness to help you learn from their examples. You will enjoy getting to know them through these pages. Michael and Bettina Jetter, Lisa Goldstein, Hobie Swan, and the entire Mindjet team—I can't thank you enough for your support and generosity. Your software is a great gift to the world.

I'd like to thank my parents Jim and Sheila Hall. They shaped my life, encouraged learning, and themselves are models of creativity. I'm grateful to my mom (who edited the manuscript before it went to the publisher), whose mastery of the English language is second to none. Finally, I'd like to thank my husband Kevin Nast. He has been there from the day I learned to create idea maps, through starting our own business in 1997, and now writing this book. I don't have the words to express my gratitude for his love, support, patience, and encouragement. He is the best!

About the Author

Jamie is committed to guiding individuals and organizations toward overcoming barriers to achieving success, including those that reside in one's own mind.

Jamie was born and raised in Fort Wayne, Indiana and currently lives in Plymouth, Michigan where she and her husband founded NastGroup, Inc., a training and consultancy organization. She has specialized in mind potential optimization since 1992. Her workshops augment mental aptitudes and maximize individual/organizational productivity. Her range of expertise spans Idea Mapping, Speed Reading, Leadership, Creating Personal Missions, Memory, Presentations, Tapping Creativity, Empowerment, Strategic Planning, Graphic Facilitation, and Learning to Learn.

In addition NastGroup works with the UK-based company, The Learning Consortium (TLC), where Jamie is a

Partner and Master Trainer. TLC is dedicated to bringing the best of all learning methods and joint client solutions to learners around the globe.

From 1992 until 2006 Jamie directed *Buzan Centres USA* and was the only Senior Master Trainer representing Buzan Centres worldwide. During that time she mentored over 15,000 people worldwide toward better mental productivity and certified 109 Qualified Buzan Instructors from 24 countries. She also wrote the *Think, Learn & Create Workshop* instructor training manual for the Buzan Centres.

She spent 12 years at Electronic Data Systems in management and leadership training capacities and was certified as a trainer for Steven Covey's *Seven Habits of Highly Effective People* in 1996. She is a graduate of Purdue University with a BA in Industrial Management and minor in Computer Science.

Using her unique, results-oriented coaching skills, Jamie brings her workshop right to the reader. She was published in the October 1996 issue of Personal Excellence and was a guest on VoiceAmerica.com in February 2004.

She is an accomplished conference speaker and has consulted for a wide array of clients including: American Institute of Banking, American Bankers Association, Association of Christian Schools International, BMC Software, BP, Chattanooga Advertising Federation, ConocoPhillips, DTE Energy, The Dwight School, Farmington Hills Public Schools, Franklin Templeton, Ford Motor Company, GM, General Physics, Institute of Management Accountants, L. L. Bean, Macomb Intermediate School District, MARC Advertising, Matrix Imaging, Mayo Clinic, Middle Tennessee State University, Mind*werx* International of Australia, Operation Smile, Pennsylvania College of Optometry, Psychotherapy Networker, Saline Leadership Institute, Software Spectrum, U.S. Army Ammunition Management, University of Pittsburgh Institute For Entrepreneurial Excellence, VHA Inc., and Willow Run High School.

Email: info@IdeaMappingSuccess.com

Phone: 866-896-1024 Toll Free or 734-207-5287 from outside the Unites States or +44(0) 1202 674676 in the United Kingdom

For more information on Idea Mapping and Jamie's workshops see www.IdeaMappingSuccess.com.

Foreword

When I think of Jamie, I think "Dedicated, practical enthusiasm!" Jamie is a wonderful combination of down to earth, no-nonsense, and "this is what really works, because I know it and I have done it"—with incredible passion.

The enthusiasm is born from 15 years of sharing these processes with busy, (often initially cynical) stressed business people and seeing them come alive again! The processes that Jamie shares are very simple and at the same time deeply profound as they are based on the way all humans process information—and they work.

This book is the culmination of all her vast experience—all her stories of people like you who needed answers to de-stressing the overloaded, overwhelmed sinking feeling so prevalent in the workplace today.

Let me speak a bit more about why Jamie should be the author of this book. Jamie was in a leadership and training organization of an information technology company and successful in her field when she attended one of the first internal classes called *Mind Matters*. That class was one of those that literally changed her life! Quickly she decided that she wanted to become a trainer to be able to teach that same class to others. This she did with great dedication to all the details. That was taken even further in that the course was changed from a video-driven course (those of you able to remember that style in the early 1990s?!) to an instructor-driven course. Jamie took on the daunting task of transcribing the videos and crafting the instructor training manual. This she did with her ability to manage minute detail while keeping the whole picture in clear focus by applying the same skills she teaches!

I was very impressed by the work she did and the final product was excellent and has now been distributed all over the world to assist new trainers in continuing to maintain the integrity of the processes.

Jamie and I worked closely together then and even more after she left her previous employer to start her own training and consultancy firm. She has earned the title of senior master trainer and was the one person in the world that I knew would carry the "Mental Literacy" torch forward just as I would (if I were to unexpectedly depart!). This was extremely gratifying.

What *Idea Mapping* brings to you are practical, immediately doable, time-saving, sanity preserving processes and templates to make your business life easier and more enjoyable! I think that will be of use to everyone I know of in the workplace today!

Tony Buzan has done a wonderful job of crafting and promulgating the Mind Map technique—what Jamie offers is that rare gift of one who has street credentials. She uses the processes herself; she has applied them over 15 years in the workplace. Further, she has taught over 14,900 people—really working with them to go from understanding to actually applying. She goes through all the "Yes, buts . . ." and "So how do I . . .?" and "I got stuck here" to assist the habit change from new skill to the effective use stage.

So, let me ask you . . .

Do you feel a bit (or a lot) overwhelmed?

Are you negatively stressed?

Do you feel even further behind at the end of the day than when you started?

Does making any kind of a presentation cause you palpitations?

Are you stuck when you are forced to come up with new ideas?

Does clear thinking seem to elude you?

Do you need to prioritize more efficiently?

Can you not turn on your thinking ability? Or can you not turn OFF your thinking ability!?

Would it be helpful if you could plan faster and better?

Would better analytical abilities be helpful?

Do you suffer from poor concentration?

Is your memory getting worse?!

Is there never enough time for what you have to do?

Do you feel unmotivated?

Is your memory getting worse??!!!!!!!

Would you like to be able to make better decisions?

Do you have problems to solve?

Are you trapped in "chicken circle" thinking?

Are you a procrastinator?

If you answered Yes! to three or more questions, then this book is for YOU!

You now hold in your hands the way to solve all those situations. You have a "Jamie-in-a-book" opportunity to have your life changed the way hers was. Better fasten your seat-belt—this will be a speed change for the better.

You'll be very pleased for the rest of your life that you started this journey.

—Vanda North

Vanda was the founder and global director of the Buzan Centres from 1988 to 2006. She is currently the founder and director of The Learning Consortium.

Preface

Are you there, buried somewhere underneath that mountain of papers and work that needs to be done? Are you overwhelmed with everything you need to accomplish? Do you have a difficult time organizing your thoughts? How would you rate your ability to create new ideas, plan, communicate your thoughts, learn, think strategically, develop and deliver presentations quickly and with excellence? If there were an easy tool that could save you time, increase your efficiency, and help you get your arms around large, complex issues (and it was fun!), would you be interested? Oh there you are! I can see you now.

Idea Mapping is a powerful tool that can help you do all this and more. This book uses a no nonsense approach to teaching a new skill to all individuals in all positions in work and life. Years ago, I picked up a book on memory—thinking that it would help me improve my own. Do you know there was nothing in that book that taught me to improve my memory? I thought, "what a waste of time." Well this book is just the opposite. There is virtually no time spent in this book on theory or fluff. In the following pages are exercises, instructions, examples, stories, processes, and applications that you can use to learn how to create idea maps.

One of the most common responses I get from people who have learned idea mapping is that they say they now think differently. Society and education have crammed our nonlinear brains into a linear box and then we wonder why learning and thinking can seem difficult at times. Idea maps capitalize on the nonlinear, associative nature of our brains. They are a reflection of how our brains are designed to work naturally.

I've had hundreds of phone calls over the years from people who wanted to learn the skill of idea mapping, but were struggling. Their line of questioning has been something like this:

"Do you have any workshops coming to my city this year?" I regretfully and frequently answer, "No."

"Where will your next workshop be held?" It usually ends up half way across the country from them.

"You know, I've read about this mapping concept, but I'm having problems getting started. Is there a book that can help me with some of my struggles and show me all the ways I can use idea mapping?" I ask them what books or materials they read. They say the books didn't help.

I wrote this book

- To provide a resource for every person who doesn't have the time or money to come to a workshop
- To transfer the skill of idea mapping from my brain to yours
- To share honestly about some of the common struggles many people have when learning this technique and to provide ways to address those challenges and make your learning easy

- To show you how you can use idea mapping in a multitude of applications
- Because every person should have the opportunity to learn how to idea map

The first five chapters will define idea mapping and walk you through how to create idea maps. You'll learn the laws of idea mapping, how to generate ideas naturally through the logic of association, the basics of getting started, some of the common obstacles to idea mapping and the solutions to those obstacles. Chapter 6 will introduce you to a dozen hand-drawn idea-mapping applications. Each will have an associated idea map and a description from its creator. Chapter 7 also covers applications, only this time the maps were all developed using Mindjet Pro 6 software. In chapter 8, three individuals share how they progressed from novice to master mapper (including examples of their maps). Chapter 9 outlines the *Team Mapping Method*—a technique for using idea mapping when groups need to generate ideas, plan, or solve problems. Chapter 10 gets to the heart of idea mapping. Now that you've mastered the laws and the basics, I'll show you some advanced mapping applications where the laws of idea mapping are broken with good reason. In Chapter 11, we will revisit an activity from Chapter 2 and compare your new mapping skills with your old linear notes. Chapter 12 gives you 28 possible idea-mapping activities for you to begin practicing. Finally, Chapter 13 gives you the ultimate challenge—"real-time" idea mapping.

I spent many years in corporate America. *Idea Mapping* combines my years of business experience, plus my years of teaching idea mapping, plus the experiences of 21 other idea mappers from around the globe. This book takes you from the beginning level and pushes you into the advanced realms of mapping. The content of the book is all about you and building your skills, and it is a privilege to share this information with you.

Welcome to your Idea Mapping Workshop! My name is Jamie Nast, and I'll be your instructor.

Introduction

"Something is happening. We are becoming a visually mediated society. For many, understanding of the world is being accomplished, not through words, but by reading images."
—Paul Martin Lester, "Syntactic Theory of Visual Communication"

Linear communication, linear thinking, linear problem solving, linear note taking—these are not reflections of how our brain was designed to process information most effectively. Sadly, linear communication is the primary tool that 98% of the world is still using in business, education, and life. From youth, we have been taught in ways that deter us from using our full spectrum of cortical skills. According to a recent article published by Hewlett-Packard, studies show that people remember 10% of what they hear, 20% of what they read, but about 80% of what they see and do. This book will teach you a revolutionary new skill that will combat underutilization of the brain and significantly improve thinking and learning by combining seeing and doing.

In today's world individuals are constantly asked to do more with less, to squeeze 12 hours of productivity into an

8-hour day, to creatively solve problems, to market new products, to continually be learning and developing professionally, to streamline processes, to plan projects that incorporate understanding and buy-in from the entire team, and to try to balance all of these things with a personal life.

Idea mapping is a revolutionary way of effectively meeting all these demands and doing so in a way that energizes you and makes you more creative than ever before. An idea map is a colorful, visual picture of the issue at hand—all on a single sheet of paper. This frees the brain to think, see, and understand in ways that cannot happen with a multipaged linear document of the same information. It breaks the tradition of linear thinking and provides a way for individuals and teams to plan, learn, increase productivity, save time, improve recall, and create using the logic of association and the full range of cortical skills.

Everyone exposed to idea mapping has found it has transformed his or her life. It works so well (seemingly miraculously) that America's major corporations, institutes, and schools have hired me to train their employees. Some of these organizations include: American Bankers Association, Association of Christian Schools International, BMC Software, BP, ConocoPhillips, DTE Energy, Franklin Templeton, Ford Motor Company, General Motors, L. L. Bean, Macomb Intermediate School District, MARC Advertising, Mayo Clinic, Middle Tennessee State University, Operation Smile, Pennsylvania College of Optometry, Saline Leadership Institute, Software Spectrum, The Dwight School, U.S. Army Ammunition Management, University of Pittsburgh Institute For Entrepreneurial Excellence, and Willow Run High School.

The associative process by which idea maps are developed is easy to learn and will be explained in Chapter 2 of this book. It mirrors how our brain naturally and freely associates information and makes connections between pieces of data. It's like having a brainstorming session with the assistance of a tool that will capture, organize, associate, and provide a comprehensive picture of those brilliant thoughts all on one page. Idea mapping eliminates the gridlock of linear thinking and nurtures the visual learner in all of us.

I graduated from Purdue University in West Lafayette, Indiana, in industrial management and computer science, and spent 12 years working as a leader for Electronic Data Systems (EDS). I was introduced to a tool called mind mapping (which I later developed into idea mapping) in 1991. My logical, analytical, and sequential brain was more than a little skeptical about its usefulness; but I also longed for a creative tool that would stimulate the right side of my brain. The ability of the idea map to integrate right and left cortex skills has produced synergistic improvements in nearly everything I do. As of this writing I have taught over 15,000 people how to idea map, certified and mentored 109 mapping instructors from 24 different countries, and have heard thousands of success stories. Some of those examples will be shared in subsequent chapters.

This book is for all individuals in all positions in work and life. I will share exceptional achievements from typical individuals around the globe. Anyone (especially you) can learn to use idea mapping to make him or herself incredibly successful! This book will show you how.

Battle of the Brains

What if there was a way to do more work with fewer resources and to reduce the number of hours spent working? What if there was a tool that could make you more efficient and more organized? What if there was a technique to enhance your creativity and your ability to communicate ideas? What if you could discover a resource that could change the very foundation of how you think and learn in a way that would enhance your work and life forever? Would you be interested?

Idea mapping has done just that for me and for millions of others around the world. It can offer the same success for you. What follows throughout this book is the process I take groups and individuals through in order to teach them to use their brains more effectively. It begins with where you are today. Here is where it began for me.

The Turning Point

It was late on a Friday afternoon in August of 1996, and I was exhausted from a month of nonstop travel delivering leadership workshops to corporate managers and supervisors of the company for which I was employed. At the time, I was working for EDS—a large, global information technology company. I was one of eight hand-selected leaders asked to join a team that develops and coaches employees throughout the Midwest and Canada in leadership competencies. On Monday the traveling would start all over again in another city. It was going to be my first time teaching a new course; however, there was a problem. I wasn't close to being prepared. It was going to be a very long weekend.

Several months earlier I had been certified as a facilitator for Stephen Covey's "The Seven Habits of Highly Effective Leaders" 5-day workshop. Since receiving the certification, I had not had the opportunity to teach the class. So not only was I unprepared, but so much time had passed in between becoming certified and being invited to speak on the topic that my memories of what I had learned were vague. Familiarizing myself with the material was going to be close to learning it all for the first time. Realistically I needed at least a week to review. If you have ever seen one of these facilitator guides, you can identify with me. It is a three-inch tome of materials (I measured my manual to be sure I wasn't exaggerating!) in addition to many videos. Along with one of my team members, I was scheduled to coteach two of these classes to two different groups in Indianapolis, Indiana, starting on Monday.

The schedule called for us to be there for 2 weeks. On Monday we were teaching the first day of class to Group A. On Tuesday we were teaching the first class to Group B. We were going to repeat that schedule until the classes were completed for both groups. As a seasoned facilitator you can fake a lot of things, but demonstrating an understanding of the material is not one of them. Maybe it was self-preservation or the desire to salvage some of my weekend, but a possible solution came to me.

I had been using and teaching individuals about a unique skill called mind mapping (mind maps® are a registered trademark of the Buzan Organization) for 4 years. (Idea mapping has its original roots in the mind mapping technique.) Mind mapping is a way of taking notes and organizing thoughts into key words and pictures and is a technique that can condense mounds of data onto one sheet of paper. It also acts as a memory tool. I knew it was powerful but had never used it for such a large (and critical) application. I was backed into a corner and had no choice. It had to work.

Here was the plan I worked out with my coworker. Since she was much more familiar with the material that we were both invited to present, she would teach day 1 to Group A. I would sit at the back of the room and map the entire day on one 11″ × 17″ sheet of paper. The following day I would teach day 1 to Group B from my map. If the process worked, we would repeat this strategy for the remainder of our time in Indianapolis. She agreed to give it a try. I enjoyed my weekend for the most part. Although I had sufficient reason to believe the plan would work, I still carried some anxiety with me to Indianapolis.

The Indianapolis experiment, as it came to be known, began on Monday as I sat in the back of the classroom with my markers, with the facilitator guide, participant manual, handouts, and the back-up set of videos surrounding me. I documented everything: sequence, stories, what page participants should turn to, whether I was using a flip chart or an overhead projector, where to cue which video, what to skip, when to eat; you name it—it went on the map. By the end of the day my brain was fried from the intense concentration, but I had done it! The next day, I taught day 1 to an unsuspecting Group B from my single 11″ × 17″ map.

Complete success! Not only did I have all the material

in front of me, but I could also see the interconnections be-tween key points. I had internalized the material fairly well, saved at least a week of preparation time, and for future classes only had to review the map before teaching. I was amazed! We executed the plan for the remainder of the workshop with equal success. I still have those original maps, and I would venture to say that I could still teach from them today—even though the last time I taught that class was in 1997.

See Figure 1.1 for the map from that first day in Indi-anapolis. (See www.IdeaMappingSuccess.com for color ver-sions of this and subsequent idea maps in this book.) I know it looks very strange, but don't worry about that at this point. You're not supposed to be able to understand my map. I just want you to begin to see how these graphical creatures are structured.

That experience personalized the magnitude of the power of mapping in a way I had not yet experienced. Since then my efficiency, productivity, and creativity have contin-ued to soar as a result of using this new skill. Now I have a reservoir of equally powerful success stories from people all around the globe. I'll share some of those throughout this book.

Objectives

This book was written with the following objectives in mind:

- To give you a tool that will help you be exponentially more productive and efficient in work and life

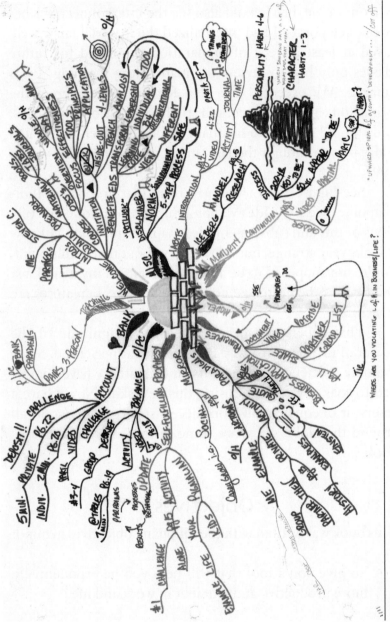

Figure 1.1 Covey Day-One Map

- To spark creative thinking
- To enable you to access the infinite expanse of your brain
- To offer an alternative to traditional thinking, communicating, creating, and learning
- To teach you the skill of idea mapping

Today's Demands On You

What business and life demands are you currently facing? In how many different directions are you being pulled? Are you constantly being asked to solve problems, be creative, plan, manage projects, save time, present ideas, keep excellent client relationships, stay on top of new information, eliminate redundancy, lead your team effectively, reduce costs, and balance that with everything else you have going on personally?

In today's busy world people are constantly being asked to do more with less. The results? People are overwhelmed. They spend huge numbers of hours at work (sometimes spinning their wheels); the job becomes this miserable albatross around one's neck; the workload only gets heavier; the boss's expectations get greater; and employees, families, and businesses all suffer. Is that how we want to live? I don't think so.

So you've turned to this book for a tool that will help you. Good choice. But here's where I want to provide a small caution. If you're like most people you have been thinking, organizing, taking notes, making decisions, planning, communicating, presenting, studying, and creating in a linear fashion since you were in elementary school. It is a deep-seated habit. You have built a strong neural pathway in your brain. It's going to take some patience, practice, and persistence to learn a new skill equally as powerful as the existing one. Idea mapping itself is not difficult to learn—in fact, it's quite simple. It's the competing tendency to return to the habit of linear notes that will take a little effort to overcome initially. For a short time it will feel easier to take notes in a linear format, but once you are through the learning curve, you will amaze yourself. Linear thinking and note taking are *normal*—but they aren't *natural*. An idea map is a *natural* reflection of how your brain was designed to work. Learning idea mapping is the first step in improving productivity, increasing creativity, and becoming more focused and organized overall. I congratulate you on your willingness to risk being different and to stray from the norm! It will be one of the best investments of time and energy you will ever make.

A Look At Your Own Notes

To understanding how idea mapping can benefit you, you must first understand how you currently externalize your thoughts onto paper. Please locate some notes you have recently taken. Preferably they are several pages in length, important, and more than 24 hours old. They can be notes you've created by hand or on the computer and for any purpose. From this point forward, I will refer to these notes as your "baseline notes."

Ask yourself the following questions:

- How well do you remember the information represented by your notes?
- How well were the thoughts organized?
- Did you use multiple colors?
- Did you include any images?
- What was your purpose for taking the notes? Did they meet your objective?
- Did you have too little or too much detail for your purpose?
- How would you rate your creativity and imagination in these pages?
- What did you do as a result of taking these notes?

This examination will give you a baseline of comparisons as you start to idea map.

Purpose of Taking Notes

The main factor I want to bring to your attention at this early stage is the importance of determining and adhering to the purpose of the notes you are taking. Often times I find people taking unnecessarily detailed notes as if they were going to be tested on the material. This habit comes from those many years of schooling. One of the best pieces of advice I can give when you are capturing your thoughts (electronically or on paper) is to define your purpose before you begin your notes. It will shape everything you do—what kind of data is captured, the amount of detail you attend to, how much time you devote to the process, the volume of material you listen to or research, how you organize your thoughts, how you determine whether it is a draft or a final product, and what the final use is for this document (or idea map!) when it is complete.

This is so important that I'm going to call it *Lesson One* in a series of lessons that will be covered in this book. (See Appendix 1 for a complete list of Lessons.)

Lesson One— Define your purpose for taking notes.

Hang on to your baseline notes. We will use them in an activity later in this book.

Benefits of Idea Mapping

Training your brain to learn more effectively will have an enormous impact on your overall efficiency. For a *trained brain*, learning requires less brain activity, while the performance outcome increases multiple times over. An *untrained brain* is a model of confusion. When asked to perform an unfamiliar task, an untrained brain will search for a solution by going to multiple parts of the brain seeking answers (and often not finding them) and is therefore inefficient. (For actual brain scans and research done at the Wake Forest University School of Medicine in Winston-Salem, North Carolina, see Chapter 9, titled "An Amazing Discovery," from *Memory Power* by Scott Hagwood.)

Ultimately idea maps can provide benefits in the following areas:

- Learning
- Creativity
- Thinking
- Planning
- Organizing
- Motivation
- FUN!!!
- Memory
- Note taking
- Decision making
- Communication
- Presentations
- Studying
- "Big Picture" view of ideas and the interrelationship between those thoughts
- Job performance
- And more!

Your job at this point is to commit to allowing me to take you through the process of learning to create idea maps. Be ready to do a bit of work. Once you've learned this new skill, I'm going to ask you to do one map each day until it feels natural for you. It will be a journey with many rewards. Ready to begin?

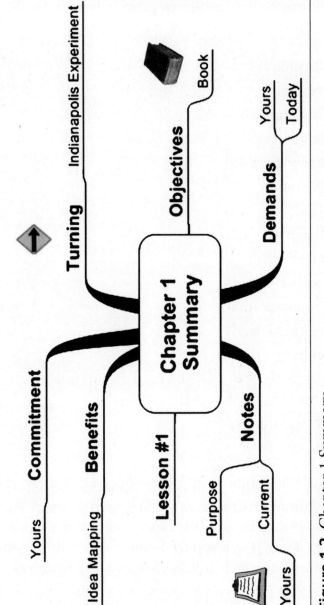

Figure 1.2 Chapter 1 Summary

Summary

There will be an idea-map summary at the end of each chapter (see Figure 1.2). I know you haven't been introduced to idea mapping yet, so let me give a brief description of Figure 1.2. At the center of this diagram is my topic—Chapter 1. The seven surrounding branches are the main ideas (for me) from the first chapter. Any additional words further define the main ideas (again for me only), and images enhance the words. You'll learn much more about this in following chapters. Use it as a review or add to it in any way that is helpful. Mostly, just be curious about it at this point and look forward to your upcoming learning.

CHAPTER

What Is an Idea Map?

This chapter will cover:

- The definition of idea mapping
- History
- Your current thought organization
- Associative thinking

Definition of Idea Mapping

"A mind map harnesses the full range of cortical skills— word, image, number, logic, rhythm, color, and spatial awareness—in a single, uniquely powerful technique. In doing so, it gives you the freedom to roam the infinite expanse of your brain."

This definition comes from Tony Buzan who is the origina- tor of mind maps and a best-selling author. Tony developed mind mapping in the late 1960s, and it is now estimated that millions of people all over the world create them in order to use their minds more effectively.

Idea mapping has a rich foundation in mind mapping and I am grateful to Tony for giving this to the world. Here is the difference. After 15 years of real-world experience and seeing business people around the world apply this tech- nique to their careers and lives, it was time for the next gen- eration—a hybrid of sorts. Idea mapping is the tool that helps many who struggle with keeping with the laws of mind mapping and who often (sadly) throw out the baby with the bath water. The laws are important to understanding so that you know when it is applicable to use them and when it is not. Thus my front-line experience with skeptical, overworked linearly trained business people has caused me to craft *idea maps* as the practical, flexible, and more usable version of mind maps. Once the rules and techniques of idea mapping are established and learned, you'll be breaking everyone of them to make these graphical works apply to you in the most effective way possible. You will be the creator of your own rules that work for you!

Now let's look back at the history even further.

History

The History of Mapping

I thought it would be fascinating for you to see some historical examples of early graphical organizers. Since the term mind mapping was not around at that time, they were referred to as tree diagrams.

In one of Ramon Llull's diagrams called the "Tree of Knowledge" (about 1270 AD) the core concept or trunk is clearly the central theme. (You will come to know this as a central image when creating your idea maps.) This theme is fully surrounded by subordinate concepts. (You will come to know these as main branches.) See Figure 2.1.

A second example of Ramon Llull's drawings also shows knowledge arranged in a tree diagram. It is called "Arbre de

Figure 2.1 The Tree of Knowledge

filosofia d'amor" ("The Tree of the Philosophy of Love"; 1298 AD). See Figure 2.2.

The graphical display of knowledge or ideas using color, lines, and association to assist human thinking was well known by medieval times. Although mapping may be a new concept to you, I think it is exciting to breathe new life

Figure 2.2 The Tree of the Philosophy of Love

into systems that have been proven over time. For this source and more historical information on graphical languages, go to www.futureknowledge.biz. Scroll down on the home page and click on "frequently asked questions." In the answer to question number one you will find Michael Cahill's (President of Future Knowledge Group, Inc.) white paper on the *History and Uses of Graphical Languages.*

My Own History

I spent the years from 1985 to 1997 working in various leadership roles for an information technology company. In my last position, where I was introduced to mind mapping, I was a management training specialist in a leadership development organization. It was an organization of top leaders assigned to teach leaders about leadership.

I first learned how to map in 1991 from a coworker. I received my formal certification in mind mapping in 1992 from Vanda North, who was previously the founder and global director of the Buzan Centres and is now the founder and director of The Learning Consortium based out of the UK. She was and continues to be a great friend and mentor. I spent the next 5 years teaching 2-day *Mind Matters* workshops throughout the United States and Canada for this employer. For many this workshop was the most impactful learning experience of their lives.

Between July 1, 1992, and June 30, 1993, 1,397 U.S. participants attended this course. A survey was sent randomly to 350 of those students with a return rate of 37%. The results were detailed, extensive, and extremely positive. It showed that 85% of the respondents applied tools from this workshop to their business/personal lives. The survey results documented a phenomenal transfer of skill from the class to the real world compared to all of the other corporate offerings. The following year the statistics were equally positive. One of the most profound results stated that 73% of the respondents said that the workshop had made a lasting impact on their business/personal lives. This was followed by three pages of quotes describing the specifics of the workshop's impact.

I witnessed many situations where the use of this tool helped leaders become incredibly successful as a result of their willingness to learn and apply this skill. My passion for this work and the exhilaration of the results continued to grow. In early 1997 this workshop and all other vendor-related courses were cut in a downsizing effort. I was at a crossroad: Do I stay with this company and do something I wouldn't enjoy? Or, do I leave, start my own company, and follow my passion to teach these skills to others? I left. It was an easy choice, and I've never looked back.

Today I combine my corporate leadership experience, my facilitation and training skills, and this wonderful tool of idea mapping to teach people all over the world.

Your Thought Organization

Let's find out how you currently organize your thoughts by imagining a situation that you have probably already experienced in some fashion. Assume you've been asked to give a presentation to a group of people and you only have 5 minutes to gather your thoughts about a particular topic. This could be the status of a project you are working on, sharing your experience in an area of expertise, updating your team on a meeting you attended, standing in for an absent presenter, or any other topic of your choice. Typically you have been given a general idea of the topic. Your assignment is to take a few minutes to choose a topic for a 30-minute presentation, create the notes that you would take to the podium, and organize them in the format and in the way you would normally do so. Take 5 minutes to create notes for this particular task before moving on. Once you have completed your notes, proceed to the next section.

Looking at these notes, again answer the questions from Chapter 1 where we reviewed your baseline notes. In addition, answer the following questions:

- How difficult was it to decide on a topic?
- Did you have moments of feeling stuck in generating your thoughts?
- How did you organize your thoughts? Were they written in sequential order? In other words, did you ask yourself "what will I say first?" Or did you generate random thoughts and organize them later?
- Could you speak from these notes for 30 minutes successfully?

A key issue to focus on within this exercise is your method of thought organization. In my experience, the majority of people use a chronological approach to generate ideas that will eventually be presented in a sequence. They focus all their effort on what to say first—not writing anything down until they get past that hurdle. Even when the outcome doesn't require a sequential outcome we respond similarly. When the purpose is to come up with the most creative solution or idea, most people will try to think of the best idea to the exclusion of any other options. This is normal linear thinking and creates barriers to our creativity and thought processes.

Let's examine this more closely by referring again to the 30-minute presentation notes created for the activity in this chapter. While your brain was focusing on what to say first, did you notice any other ideas popping into your brain? Probably. When these other creative ideas came to mind what did you do? What usually happens is these out of sequence thoughts don't get captured because people feel compelled to start at the beginning and work their way through to the end in a linear process. This is similar to the trap people can fall into when reading a book. Many feel they must read from page one and go all the way to the end—even if they find they don't like the book shortly after starting— even if data is only needed from a few chapters. (In this book, please give yourself permission to read in any order and in any quantity that is best for your purpose.)

By the time you reach the point in your notes where the other ideas (the ones you had before you were ready to have them) would have been beneficial, they're gone—forgotten! These ideas could have shaped the initial part of your presentation and made creating what you would say first much easier. Instead we spent more time getting inferior results. This is one of the problems with using a chronological or linear approach.

Associative Thinking

Let's look at two ways the brain creates associations. The first method is called a bloom of associations (BrainBloom™ process developed by Vanda North). This is a process in which all ideas are generated from and associated to a central thought.

All associations radiate from a central idea. The second method is called a flow of associations. In this case, the association begins with a single thought that leads to another thought, which leads to another thought. It's like a long stream of consciouness.

The creation of an idea map combines the bloom and flow of associations. Following are three activities that will demonstrate the bloom, the flow, and the bloom plus flow of associations.

Activity #1—Bloom of Ideas

Idea mapping uses the logic of association in creating its structure. It also combines this with chronology, but that comes after the ideas have been generated. Let's do an activity that will better demonstrate what is meant by the logic of association.

Take a sheet of blank paper and write a word in the center of the page. You can use any single word or use my example in Figure 2.3. Off of this word, draw 10 blank lines.

On the lines, write the first 10 single words that come to mind when you think of the word in the middle. This process represents a *bloom* of thought. These 10 words *associate* to the central word.

Activity #2—Flow of Ideas

Next we'll do something a bit different. Again start with a single word of your choosing or use mine in Figure 2.4. Draw a line from your word, another branch from that one, and so forth, until you have 10.

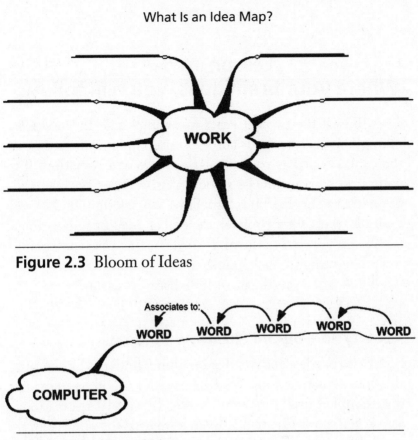

Figure 2.3 Bloom of Ideas

Figure 2.4 Flow of Ideas

Beginning with the first line off of *computer*, write the first word that comes to mind when you think of the word *computer*. On the next line write the first word that comes to mind when you think of the word you just wrote down. Follow this pattern until you've completed 10 words. This represents a *flow* of thought. Each word *associates* to the previous word.

So far we've differentiated between blooming and flowing. Here's the next critical lesson. It applies to capturing ideas as your brain creates thoughts.

Lesson Two—
Where your brain goes, you will follow.

Let's look at the two activities just completed. In the *bloom* example, I imagine it was hard to stay completely focused on the central word as your primary source of association. It's natural to start a flow of associations at times because the brain just can't help it! It is associative in its design. In the *flow* example, there were probably several choices of associations each time you wrote down a word. In this case our brains were blooming at each point, and we simply selected the word that stood out the most for whatever reason.

Activity #3—Bloom Plus Flow of Ideas

So let's do one last activity that combines both the bloom and the flow of associations. Go back to your bloom activity. In my example I used the word *WORK*. I made 10 associations as you can see in Figure 2.5. Even if we used the same central word, I doubt we had many associations in common because our experiences and associations with this word are different.

Lesson Three—
Two individuals' idea maps on an
identical topic will look different.

This time add single-word associations to your original bloom activity. Look at the central word plus the 10 surrounding words. When the first word associating to any of

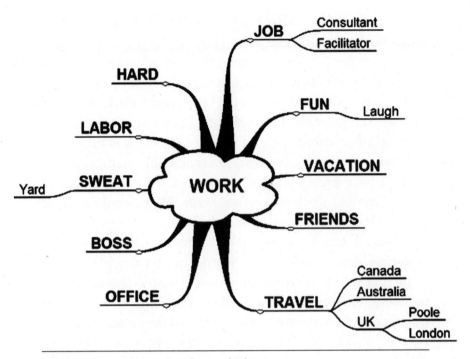

Figure 2.5 Bloom + Flow of Ideas

these 11 words (including the word *WORK*) comes to mind, draw a line connecting to the associating word and write your new word on that line. See the following example using the word *WORK* as the central thought. Words will come to you randomly. Go where your mind takes you. Let the ideas come naturally. You will be blooming and flowing at the same time—a natural reflection of how the brain works! Spend 3 or 4 minutes allowing this process to work. If you have a question about where a word should go, ask yourself, "To what branch does my new word connect?" That's where you draw a new line and then write the word on that line.

Let me explain what I did in Figure 2.5. When I did my initial bloom around the word *WORK,* the words I thought of were *job, fun, vacation, friends, travel, office, boss, sweat, labor,* and *hard.* I don't know why those were the first 10 words that came to mind—they just were. However, I do know what each word represents. I thought of *job* because it's a synonym for work. *Fun* came to mind because my work is extremely fun. I also need rest from work, so that made me think of *vacation.* I have great *friends* with whom I work. My *office* is a mess. Physical work makes me *sweat.* Work could also be called *labor,* and sometimes work is *hard.*

Next I asked you to make additions to your original bloom of ideas. I added more words (in no particular order) to further define the existing words. I added *consultant* and *facilitator* to describe portions of my job, *laugh* to expand on what I consider to be part of fun, a few of the locations where I travel, and finally I sweat when working in the *yard.* It's very important to understand that I broke this process into two phases to teach you the difference between blooming and flowing. If I had been creating an idea map, I would not complete the bloom before allowing myself to add sub-ideas. I would add ideas as I thought of them—regardless of where they would be positioned in the map.

Soon you will be using this technique to create and deliver presentations, keep track of what needs to be done, plan meetings, develop marketing strategies, dissect a complex problem, and do many, many more applications.

You have experienced how the brain generates ideas associatively in the bloom and flow activities. The best strategy for capturing ideas comes back to Lesson Two—"Where your brain goes, you will follow." This lesson applies even when generating thoughts for an application that will require chronology in the final draft. An idea map will provide the structure in which you can organize and sequence ideas despite their random creation. Generating ideas for a task where the eventual outcome will require chronology brings us to another lesson:

Lesson Four—
Just capture ideas. Order comes later.

The associative process is the logic by which an idea map is created. It is a natural reflection of how the brain works. See Figure 2.6 for my summary of this chapter in an idea map. You're now ready to look at the laws of idea mapping, learn how to read an idea map, and start creating one of your own.

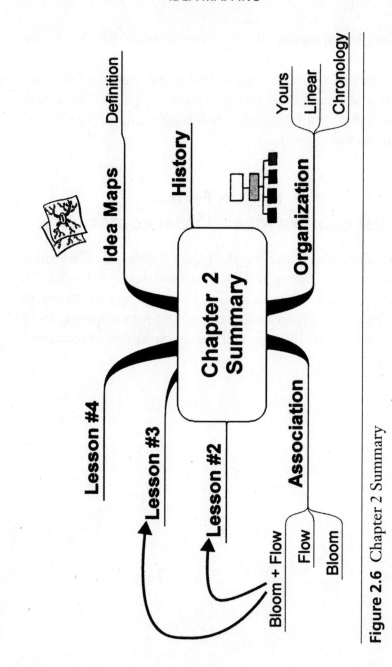

Figure 2.6 Chapter 2 Summary

3

Reading and Creating Idea Maps

I n this chapter you will:

- Review the laws of idea mapping
- Learn how to read an idea map
- See how an idea map is developed
- Create your first idea map

The Laws of Idea Mapping

The word *laws* as it is used here can be misleading if taken out of context. After all, this is a tool to tap into your creativity! These rules are *not* meant to restrict your creativity or thinking. Just as traffic laws help us travel safely from point to point, these laws are meant to be guidelines that will maximize the power of your mind through the idea map, rather than restrictions or obstacles that hinder your ability to use this tool. These laws will provide you with the resources, tips, and freedom to explore your infinite brain capacity. Once you have developed a strong habit of following the laws, you can make deliberate choices to break them based on your purpose and flair for artistic interpretation! You'll see specific examples of this in Chapter 10! In the meantime, let's first master the basics.

Lesson Five—
Starting position:
Follow the laws—for now.

The laws of idea mapping reflect the strengths of the cortical skills on both sides of the brain. Now you will have a whole-brain tool that will enable you to integrate logic, lines, words, lists, numbers, and sequence with color and images. Best of all, the right side of the brain loves the gestalt of having everything on one sheet of paper and seeing the interconnections between ideas.

So let's review these laws and at the same time learn how to read an idea map. You will need a set of colored pencils or markers that won't bleed through the paper in this book. Refer to Figure 3.1 as the laws are described. The topic of this idea map is The Laws of Idea Mapping. For a colored version of this and all subsequent idea maps go to www.IdeaMappingSuccess.com.

How to Read an Idea Map

Central Image

With all idea maps, the creation of the map begins in the center. The central image or word–image combination represents the topic or theme of your idea map. It should contain at least three colors so that it is visually memorable. The central image in Figure 3.1 is a stack of idea maps. Use at least three different colored pencils, highlighters, or markers and

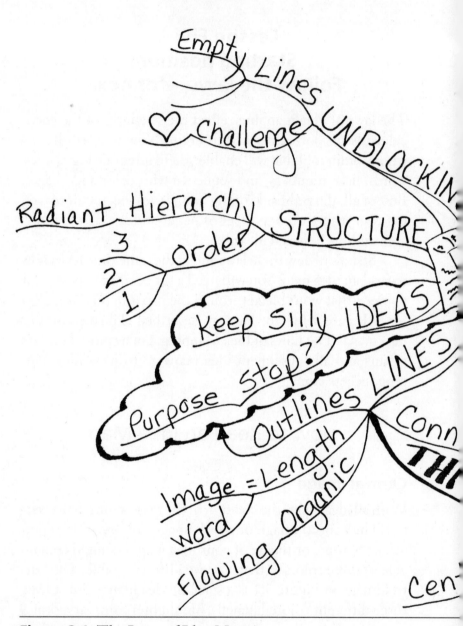

Figure 3.1 The Laws of Idea Mapping

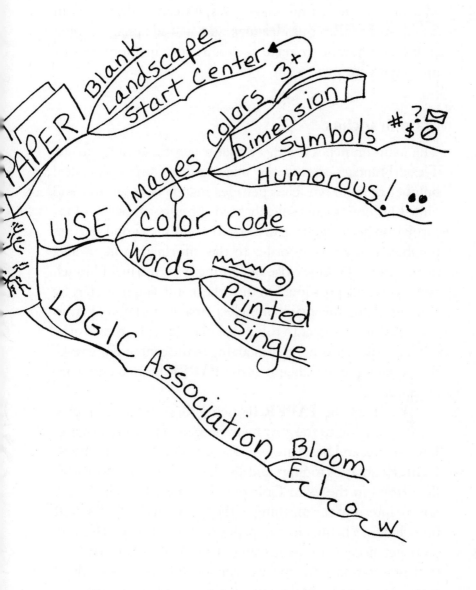

add color to the central image. (Yes, it's OK to draw in your book!) As I explain this idea map, you will add images, color, codes, and humor to make the map more memorable—by making it your own.

Main Branches

The main branches are those that touch the central image. These branches signify the major subject areas. An ideal number of main branches per idea map is between five and nine. Our brains can typically hold about seven pieces of information before getting distracted, so this is a good starting number. If there is an order to the information in an idea map, you read it clockwise beginning with the main branch at the 1 o'clock position. On the otherhand, you may start by reading all of the main branches first in order to get an overview of the topic. In this particular example, there isn't a critical sequence other than starting in the center. For ease of the explanation, let's begin at the **PAPER** branch and work clockwise.

You read the **PAPER** branch and all its subbranches before going on to the next main branch. The words **Blank, Landscape,** and **Start** are associated with the word **PAPER**. **Center** associates to **Start** and also has a connection (through the arrow) to the word **Colors** on the next branch. Here's how to interpret the meaning of the key words in the **PAPER** branch: Use a blank piece of paper turned sideways. (It's easier to get more on the page using a landscape rather than portrait orientation.) Start in the center and use at least three colors to draw a central image. For 8.5" × 11" paper the central image should be roughly two inches in diameter. You will apply these guidelines at the end of this chapter when you make your first map.

Still referring to Figure 3.1, take another pencil or marker and color in the thick part of the **PAPER** branch. Continue coloring over all the subbranches (not the words) connected to this branch using the same marker. The words are both physically and visually connected through color and lines. Again, using the same color you used on the idea map, you may want to highlight or underline the bolded words (**PAPER, Blank, Landscape, Start, Center,** and **Colors**) in the previous paragraph. This will help to visually tie the idea map to the text of this book through color.

The next branch at the 3 o'clock position is **USE**. Idea maps use **Images, Color,** and **Words. Images** have **Color** and **Dimension** to make them stand out. **Symbols** make good **Images** as well. Any time you can make the **Images Humorous** you will add enjoyment, which creates better re-call. **Color** is used throughout the idea map and can be used as your personal **Code.** Words should be **Single Key Words** that are **Printed** on the lines.

With a different color than you used for the **PAPER** branch, color in the thick part of the **USE** branch, and con-tinue highlighting over the tops of its subbranches. On the **Symbols** branch, add a couple of symbols or icons using a variety of colors. Add images to any part of this idea map as it pleases you. Images can include anything that enhances your recall. For example, you could add a flower over the **Bloom** branch, or try using the "l" in **Bloom** as the stem of the flower. Add a rainbow of colors over the **Colors** branch or a ruler to the **Length** branch. Be creative.

The **LOGIC** branch is at the 5 o'clock position. Idea

maps use the logic of **Association** through the **Bloom** and **Flow** of ideas covered in Chapter 2. Choose a new color to fill in the **LOGIC** branch and its subbranches.

LINES (branches, subbranches, and arrows) are **Connected** and **Organic.** Main branches are **Thicker** where they touch the image in the **Center.** The **Length** of the line should be the same as the length of the **Word** or **Image** sitting on the line. The idea here is to avoid wasting space or creating visual disconnects with long lines and short words. Finally you may find you want to **Outline** a branch to make it stand out or to differentiate it from a neighboring branch if things get a bit crowded. Instead of an actual line around the whole branch, I've seen people use crayons or light colored pencils to shade over the branch. Choose a new color for the **LINES** branch. You know the drill now.

IDEAS—this branch is at the 8 o'clock position. When do you **Stop** the flow of **IDEAS**? That's a personal choice based on the **Purpose** of your map. **Keep** all your **IDEAS** in your idea map, even if they seem **Silly.** Don't edit. They may provide the creative spark that leads you to another brilliant idea. Color in this branch with a new color. If you run out of colors, don't hesitate to repeat some favorites!

Idea maps have a **Radiant STRUCTURE** (10 o'clock) that builds ideas from the inside out. The most important ideas in the **Hierarchy** are in the central image followed by the main branches. Then work your way out to the smallest detail branches. The **Order** of the branches on this idea map is clockwise, so on the left hand side of the map the sequence of ideas is from the bottom up . . . **1–2–3.** Color the entire **STRUCTURE** branch.

The last branch at 11 o'clock is **UNBLOCKING.** If

you get stuck or forget the word you were going to add, draw **Empty Lines** off the branch in question to indicate where you want to make the addition. Our brain loves the **Challenge** to complete, and by just moving on, 99% of the time the idea will eventually resurface. This phenomenon is similar to struggling to recall a piece of known information such as someone's name or the title of a movie. Several minutes or hours later, you might be doing a completely different activity when all of a sudden you recall the data. Color this branch with a new color.

This description of the laws and how to read an idea map took several pages of linear text. Isn't it fascinating to see that same information (Figure 3.1) on one piece of paper with your additions of color and imagery? Now it's time to show you how an idea map is created using these laws and the power of association.

Developing an Idea Map

Figures 3.2, 3.3, and 3.4 provide an incremental demonstration of the steps to developing an idea map. This series of examples represents building a map of my current "To-Do" list. It includes both personal and professional tasks. Refer to these figures as you follow along with the description of how the final idea map was developed. I have incorporated the blooming and flowing association techniques described in Chapter 1.

Look at Figure 3.2. In this idea map, I started with a central image that represents my typical to-do list. The first idea that came to mind was the **MEETING** I was going to have at **Noon** with **Kevin.** The next thought was the **STOPS**

Figure 3.2 Idea Map Part I

I could make while I was out. Notice that I used the 7 o'clock position for this branch rather than working my way around clockwise. When there is no sequence to the idea map, I recommend visually balancing the placement of the branches around the central image. This approach leaves room for additional branches and helps to avoid ending up with a lopsided map.

Now look at Figure 3.3. As thoughts came to mind, I added more specifics to the **STOP** branch at **Costco**, an-

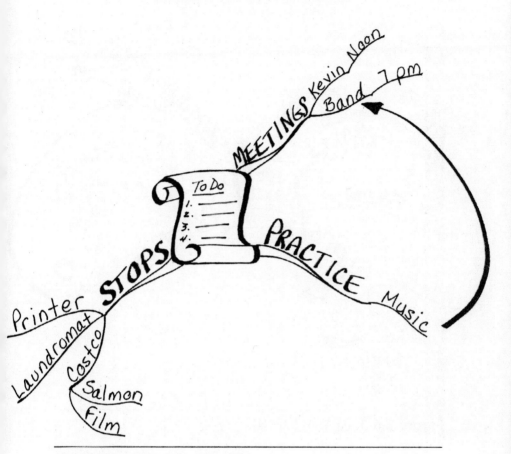

Figure 3.3 Idea Map Part II

other **MEETING,** and a branch for **PRACTICE** at the 5 o'clock position. By using an arrow, a relationship was created between the **Music** I need to practice and the **Band** rehearsal at **7 PM.**

Finally look at Figure 3.4. Here I added a new branch for **CALLS** at the 11 o'clock position, plus two additional main branches, more details, and a couple of icons. The ideas

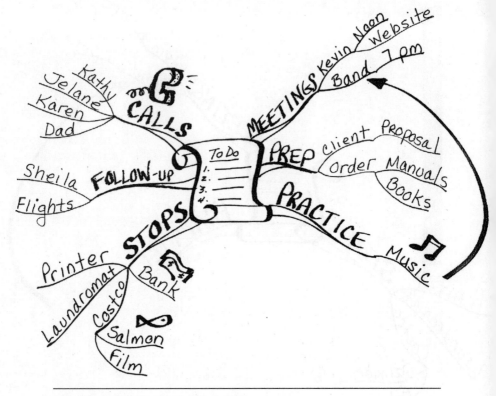

Figure 3.4 Idea Map Part III

were added in no particular order. They simply went into the map as they came to my mind.

You may be thinking, "It would be faster to create my normal list." At this stage of your learning, you may be right. However, I think you will notice a couple of things.

1. Most people are buried in random messages, sticky notes, and lists of action items. Whether these are electronically generated or handwritten, they are typically

housed in a variety of places and lack organization. Creating an idea map will enable you to embrace all these tasks and organize your thoughts on one piece of paper.

2. Secondly, when learning a new skill it is best to start small and work your way up to more challenging levels of competence. I will incrementally build on your learning rather than overwhelm you right from the beginning. Such is the main objective of this activity. We'll progress to more challenging idea maps in later chapters.

By using your natural ability to associate, it is amazing the number of items you can remember. It's fun, more visually appealing, and you can still check off the completed tasks!

Creating Your Own Idea Map

Now it's your turn to create one for yourself. Start with a topic that's easy and familiar. This way the focus can be on creating the idea map rather than determining the content of the map. Use your to do list, an agenda for a meeting, or anything else that seems relatively easy.

Using a set of colored markers, preferably with fine tips, create a central image in the middle of a blank piece of paper, and remember to turn your paper to the landscape orientation. Let your mind have a party as it jumps from idea to idea. Don't worry about perfection. This is just an opportunity for you to practice! When you are at a stopping point, sit back and admire your work ☺! See Figure 3.5 for a summary of this chapter.

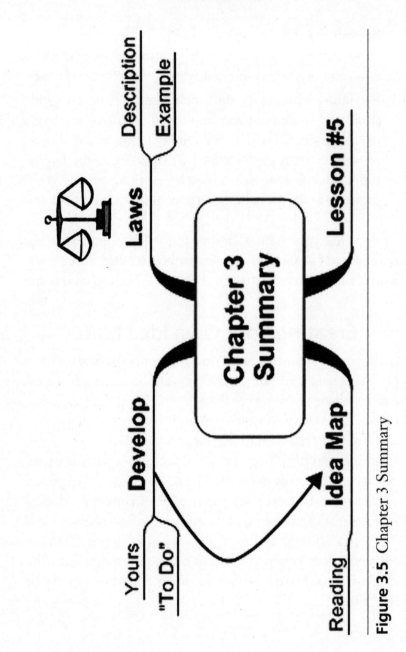

Figure 3.5 Chapter 3 Summary

4

The Three Basics of Idea Mapping

Creating idea maps requires mastering three basic, fundamental skills and then applying them. They are:

1. Identifying key words.
2. Creating main branches.
3. Drawing simple icons.

Once you have developed these skills you can create idea maps with ease. Your proficiency in creating idea maps then becomes a function of practice. You will work through a series of activities to learn more about each of these skills.

Identifying Key Words

One of the laws of idea mapping referenced in Chapter 3 explained the rationale behind the use of one single key word per branch. While nearly 90% of text is comprised of non-essential words (like of, the, at, and, in, a, was, etc.), an idea map uses only the essential words (and images) necessary for you to meet your objective or purpose for taking or making notes. Read the following paragraph. Underline or circle what you consider to be the key words for you.

Born February 11, 1847, Thomas Edison was an inventor and a scientist. At that time electricity was thought of as a fad. By the time he died in 1931, entire cities were being lit by electricity. Edison patented over 1,000 inventions. His most fa-

mous invention was an incandescent light bulb. Edison improved upon the original designs of the stock ticker and the telephone. He developed the phonograph and the kinetoscope, a box for viewing moving films. He created his most significant and far-reaching invention between 1883 and 1884 when he introduced the world's first system of centrally generated and distributed electric heat, light, and power. He believed in hard work, sometimes working 20 hours a day. Edison was quoted as saying, "Genius is 1 percent inspiration and 99 percent perspiration."

Add up the number of individual key words you circled and give yourself a total. It will probably be somewhere in the range of 6 to 36 words. The quantity of key words identified in any situation will depend on a variety of factors, including your familiarity with the material, the amount of detail you need to capture, your purpose and level of interest, and how much you trust your memory. I find that many people take notes as if they are going to be tested on the material rather than pick out the information that is important to them. Therefore, the tendency is to have more words in the map than necessary. It is perhaps more difficult to see this in the previous example because it's a generic activity and there's no defined purpose. It will be easier to demonstrate this in a real situation. For now just be aware of why you highlighted or circled your particular words.

Benefits of Using Key Words

The most obvious advantage of using fewer words is that it saves space. Therefore, much more information is contained in an idea map where key words—rather than phrases or sentences—relay an idea. It is also much easier to see the relationship between thoughts. Key words provide a foundation of words and thoughts for you to choose from when creating your idea map. Just because you circled a word does not guarantee that it will be included in your eventual map. Based on your purpose you may decide to exclude or even change the word to something more meaningful to you.

Choosing key words from written material is different than identifying them in the moment while in a meeting or conference. You need to be mentally present in order to decide how to condense a thought or a phrase into a single word. The benefit of this is that the added pressure helps you to stay focused and naturally alert during the mapping process and encourages you to ask the question, "What does this mean to me?" You are listening, internalizing, and making decisions about where to place the key words in the map—all at the same time. This adds up to greater learning and recall.

Key Words—Your Own Notes

The most conducive scenario for determining key words is when you are externalizing your own thoughts. This practice is similar to the one used in the idea map you created at the end of Chapter 3. For a final exercise on determining key words, return to your baseline notes from Chapter 1. These are the linear notes I asked you to keep under the heading "A Look at Your Own Notes." Briefly review these notes and remind yourself of your purpose for capturing this information. Why did you keep these notes? What future purpose will they serve? Now, if you know that you don't need to refer to these notes again, please throw them away (after the next exercise). However, if you need to keep them, the following exercise may reinforce the importance and recall of the information.

Similar to what you did in the paragraph about Thomas Edison, highlight or circle the key words in your notes. The purpose this time should be much clearer because you—using your notes—have defined it. Once you have identified the key words, keep these notes available and we will revisit them in another activity later in the chapter.

Identifying Main Branches

Once you've chosen a word to include in your idea map, the next challenge is deciding if it is a main branch or a subbranch. Again, five to nine main branches is an ideal number to include within the map. The best way to illustrate how this works is to complete a practice activity. The purpose of this activity is to teach you how to determine main branches and subbranches. Your assignment is to create an idea map from the following list of key words using *WORK* as the central theme:

Travel	Desk	Boss	Computer
Telephone	Colleague	Proposal	Salary
Commute	Interview	Goals	Office
Holidays	Commission	Customer	Staff
Overtime	Position	Challenge	Projects
Coffee	Hours	Meeting	Team
Mission	Job	Product	Training
Competencies	Leadership	Success	Schedule
Website	Values	Benefits	Aspirations
Vacation	Coaching	Delegate	Bonus

Put the word *WORK* (or an image that represents work) in the center of your paper, and remember to turn your paper sideways (landscape). Scan the listed words and choose a main branch that could hold two or more of these words as subbranches. The title of your main branch (or subbranches) may or may not be among these words. For example, I might choose the word *People* as one of my main branches. It's not in the list, but when I see words like *staff, colleague, boss, team,* and *customer,* I think *People* would describe this branch well. This grouping of words is a personal choice. You may have an entirely different way of categorizing the words. Choose the way that makes the most sense to you. You may consider using highlighters or symbols (boxes, circles, stars) to determine categories on this chart prior to drawing your idea map.

Draw each main branch on your idea map and then connect all the associated words from the list on subbranches or sub-subbranches. As you add words to your idea map, cross them off the list and continue the process until all words are used somewhere in the map. See Figure 4.1 for an example of how I might organize these words into an idea map.

Continuing with Your Notes

Let's go back to your baseline notes again. You already identified the key words. Now it's time to begin building an idea map of these notes. Start with a blank sheet of paper and draw a central image. Review the key words you highlighted and determine the main branches. Remember just because you highlighted a key word it does not mean that it must go in the idea map, and you may need to create a main branch to hold some of the key words. This might mean coming up

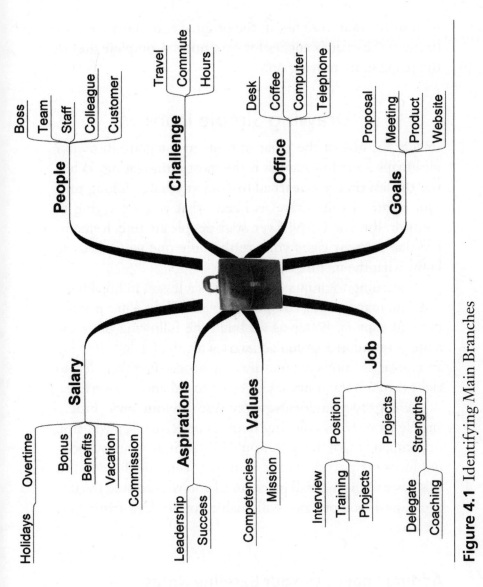

Figure 4.1 Identifying Main Branches

with words that were not in the original text. Take the time to create the main branches for your notes. Complete the entire map before moving on.

Drawing Simple Icons

Imagery is one of the greatest tools to integrate into your idea maps—yet for many it is the most intimidating. When was the last time you learned to draw anything? A long time ago, right? "I can't draw" is likely what you are saying to yourself. But you CAN! Even stick people are fine. Remember that in most cases you are the only one who needs to know what the picture represents.

Learning to draw simple icons is a lesson in breaking a task into manageable, component pieces. Take a piece of paper and copy each step as we build the following three examples found in Figure 4.2. Start with the far left drawing and make additions to your drawing proceeding from left to right through the frames. Use color to enhance the images.

How did you do? Now try one on your own. Find a simple icon (from coloring books, comic strips, a website, or company logo) that you would like to draw. Start by looking for some portion of the icon that seems doable. Add to this basic shape in small pieces until you've recreated the image. Continued practice will enable you to draw from your memory.

Adding Images to Your Baseline Notes

Let's revisit your baseline notes and idea map one last time. So far you selected key words, created main branches, and

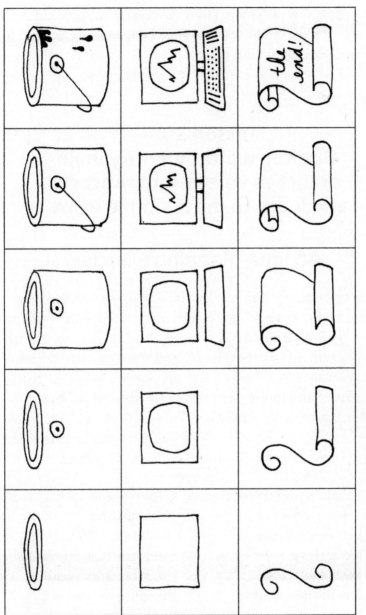

Figure 4.2 Drawing Simple Icons

completed your idea map. Does the current map include any images? Where could you add a symbol, code, or picture to enhance your recall and increase your interest in this information? Add your own images to this map now.

Lesson Six—
Use key words, identify main branches versus subbranches, and learn to draw simple icons.

An Idea-Mapping Exercise

Using your baseline notes, I walked you through the incremental steps to creating an idea map from your existing notes. Now it's time to put these basic skills (combined with the laws learned in previous chapters) into practice by completing an activity for which written notes may not currently exist. From this point forward, your idea maps should be practical applications that will be useful to you. Here are some of the tasks for which idea mapping can be extremely useful. Use this as a springboard for your own ideas.

Creating and delivering
   a presentation
Problem solving
Job interview
Strategic plan
Decision making
Personal vision/mission

Group or individual
   brainstorm
Book review
Study for certification or
   further education
Planning of any kind

Getting your arms around complex data
Customer profile
Project
Meeting agenda
Performance review
Phone call
Career plan
Organizational vision/ mission

Job description
Notes on an important article or document
Difficult conversation
Develop or deliver training
Negotiating
Marketing

Before reading Chapter 5, create one or two idea maps that will help you with a specific task, challenge, decision, project, or issue you are currently facing. See Figure 4.3 for a summary of this chapter in an idea map.

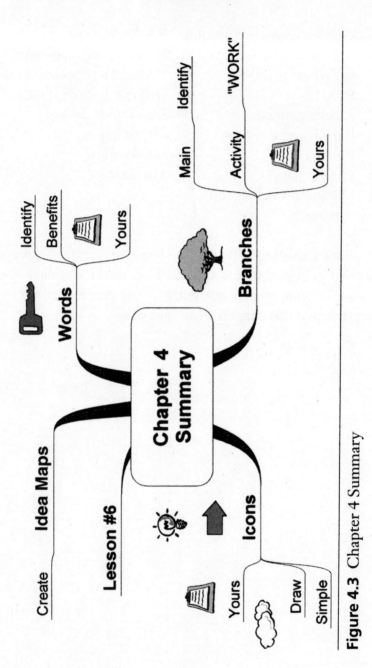

Figure 4.3 Chapter 4 Summary

5

Detours

The purpose of this chapter is to eliminate any potential learning barriers by providing solutions for the most common struggles individuals encounter when learning to create idea maps. These obstacles include:

- One Word Per Line
- Writing Upside Down
- Line Connections
- Markers & Paper
- Main Branch versus Sub-Branch
- Level of Detail
- Looking for Perfection on the First Draft
- Running Out of Room & Paper
- Images
- "Real-Time" Idea Mapping
- The Idea Generation Process

Reading a book to learn a new skill is the next best thing to attending a workshop where there is immediate feedback and coaching. However, sometimes a book leaves unanswered questions that can slow down or limit learning. Becoming your virtual teacher, standing over your shoulder, bringing you into my vast experience of addressing typical questions, and helping you to avoid pitfalls—that is one of the main goals of this book. This chapter brings the idea-mapping workshop directly to you. It covers the most frequent struggles people have when learning to create idea maps—and numerous solutions to those challenges.

During the first few attempts to create idea maps you may have already faced a few of these dilemmas. The objective now is to help you minimize the learning obstacles and to create strong habits that will maximize your success in business and life. Let's begin with the most common difficulty:

Obstacle #1— One Word Per Line

Detour #1—"I'm having a hard time condensing thoughts into one word per line. What if I need to use more than one word?" I've heard this question thousands of times. To address this let's examine why the struggle is so common, the advantage of using one word per line, and when to break the law.

The habit for most people is to write in phrases, sentences, bullet points, or outlines. Not only have you been doing it for a long time, but it is your normal habit AND you are good at it. Learning to boil thoughts down into single words is going to feel awkward for a while. Keep persisting!

Refer to Chapter 2 and look at your bloom activity around the word *WORK*. Imagine for a moment that the central topic changed from that single word to the phrase *WORKING ON A REPORT*. Picture the associations you would make while blooming ideas around this topic. Notice how the scope of these ideas is limited by using a central phrase instead of a word. Where the single word *WORK* generates many more possibilities and gives more flexibility. When the purpose for making notes is creating, brainstorming ideas, planning, or solving problems, adhering to one word per line will allow for more freedom for your thoughts to explore possibilities.

Lesson Seven— A single key word generates more thoughts than a phrase.

Still struggling? I know. It's a challenge to break old habits. Here are a few more suggestions. Consider how you could boil the following phrases into key words and images:

- Finish budget for project
- Update project plan and distribute to team
- Pack boxes with seven instruction manuals
- Send boxes to William in Japan

Try substituting an image for a phrase, or use a word/image combination. Ask yourself, "If any of these words were eliminated, would I still understand the meaning?" Remember these idea maps only need to be understood by you. See Figure 5.1 for how I might put these first two phrases onto a branch.

Notice all of the unimportant words I eliminated. I didn't lose the meaning of needing to finish the budget. I know I need to finish it. There was no reason to include team either. Who else would I send the plan to anyway? Let's look

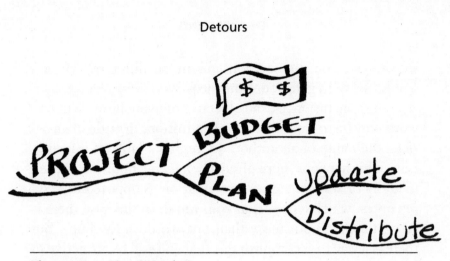

Figure 5.1 Key Words I

Figure 5.2 Key Words II

at one more example. See Figure 5.2 for how I might put the last two phrases onto a branch.

In this case the box represents the idea that I need to both pack and ship. That eliminated most of the extra words. There are many different ways to accomplish minimizing words, and your associations might be different. My examples serve to give you some ideas.

In some instances, the objective of using more than one word may be to capture a literal definition, the title of an article, the name of an author, quotes, or a table of information. This happens more often when *taking* notes on written material or someone else's presentation as opposed to *making* notes, which come from your mind. In this case there is an argument to put more than one word on the line—but there is a way to accomplish this that will still be attractive to both sides of your brain!

In the case where you want to include a diagram or table of information, create a main branch and put the name of the table or chart on that branch. In Figure 5.3 I called the branch Table XYZ. Then attach the whole table as its subbranch by inserting a copy of the table or recreating it by hand. If you need to expound upon any information in this table, color-code the relevant parts of the table to match the branch(es) that will contain more detail. For book titles and authors, draw an image of the book on the branch (or as the central image) and write the title and/or author on the book. It may be more than one word, but it still looks like an image. For definitions and quotes create subbranches that look like cartoon bubbles with the text inside. Add images and color. It's more visually appealing and more memorable than writing a sentence. These are some examples of when and how to work around the one-word-per-line dilemma. You will discover additional creative solutions to suit your own needs. See Figure 5.3 for visual support of these examples.

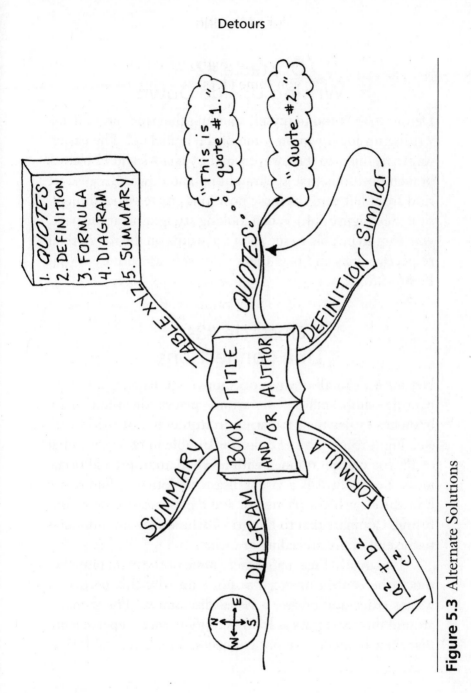

Figure 5.3 Alternate Solutions

Obstacle #2—
Writing Upside Down

Detour #2—"I found myself spinning the paper around and writing upside down on some of the branches." The easiest way to fix this is to stay away from the 6 o'clock and 12 o'clock branch positions that go straight up and down. Because we read from left to right these positions create visual difficulties. (See Figure 5.4.) When looking straight on at the page, you want to be able to see all of the words on the top of their respective lines and read them right-side up with ease. (See Figure 5.5.)

Obstacle #3—
Line Connections

Detour #3—In all of my workshops I see participants connecting subbranches to various places on their main branches rather than radiating from the end of the branch (see Figure 5.6). This is cause for trouble in two ways. First of all, you can get trapped with nowhere to insert additional ideas. Secondly, it is a visual disaster. Notice in Figure 5.6 how the clear hierarchy is lost and the associations get confusing. Compare that to Figure 5.7 where each line connects to the end of the preceding branch.

Frequently I see maps where none of the main branches touch the central image. I'm not sure why this occurs. It wastes space and creates a visual disconnect. The scenario around this issue goes as follows. I point out to a participant that their branches are not connected to the central image.

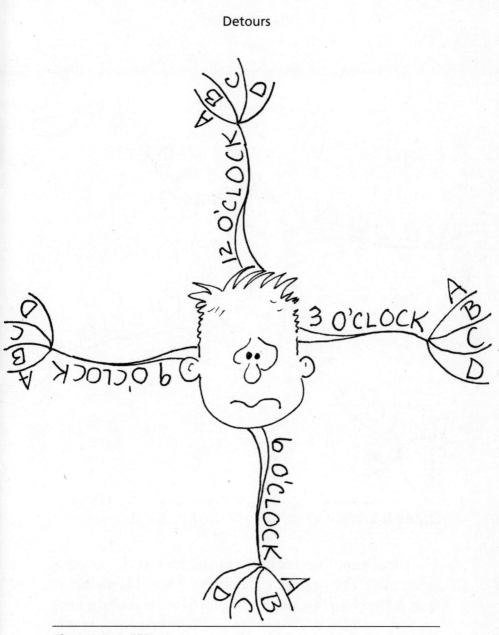

Figure 5.4 Wrong

Figure 5.5 Right

The participant fixes the problem and later works on a different map. The next time I look over his or her shoulder, there is a circle or box around the central image, and the lines are now touching the box or circle. We're making progress, but again it's a waste of space, and this technique will make all central images look similar—an image inside a box or

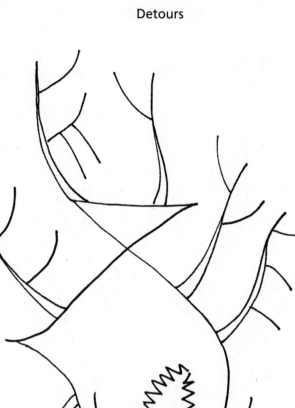

Figure 5.6 Wrong

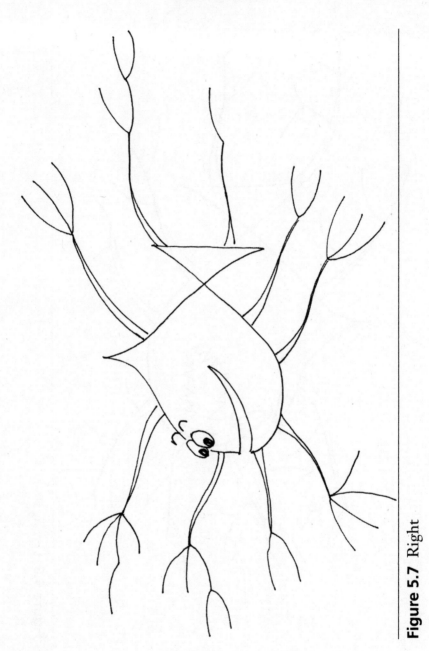

Figure 5.7 Right

circle. You want unique central images. I point out the box issue. The participant finally gets it! Let your main branches connect to the central image!

Here's my last observation about lines. Occasionally individuals will draw a line, but will not put a word on the line. Instead, he or she leaves the line blank and writes the word beginning at the end of the branch. You see this line, word, line, word pattern. This is the ultimate waste of space, so avoid it. Okay, enough about lines.

Obstacle #4— Markers & Paper

Detour #4—"These markers draw lines that are too fat or too skinny. The markers bleed through or smear on the paper. I can't imagine carrying my markers into a meeting with a client!" Having the right tools for the job (and ones you are comfortable with) is essential for success. Different situations will require a variety of tools.

I have become a markeraholic, so let me pass along some advice. Everyone has their own preferences, but I suggest a minimum of ten colors and a set of both extra fine and medium fine tips. There are also several manufacturers that produce markers with a different tip on each end. The sets that come with cases make them easier to carry. Don't buy a cheap pack of twenty-four colors from a dollar store—the markers that do work probably won't make it through a second day. If you don't want to carry your markers around, I suggest a four-color pen. Just be careful to change colors quietly when you are in a group or the clicking may be distracting to others! You probably haven't had the thrill of shopping for colored markers since childhood, so enjoy it!

Next is the paper. Find a notebook or create one with paper that is heavy enough to handle any marker bleeding. I frequently use blank copy paper. For more formal idea maps I have an 8.5″ × 11″ sketchpad, and when out of the office I carry a small binder that holds my PDA, a four-color pen, and blank paper folded in on itself (so the paper, when unfolded, is twice the size of the binder.)

Obstacle #5— Main Branch versus Subbranch

Detour #5—"I'm having trouble deciding which word should act as the main branch versus a detail branch." Here's an example: The central topic is planning for a business trip. In this scenario, the words *clothes* and *packing* are going into the map. They will both be part of the same-colored branch, but the question is which word should be on the main branch and which one should be subordinate. Mentally picture putting *clothes* on the main branch and *packing* linked as a subbranch. Imagine how many other ideas you could generate from the word *clothes* in addition to *packing*. Now start over and mentally reverse the position of the two words. Imagine how many ideas you could generate from the word *packing* in addition to *clothes*. Does using *packing* as the main branch generate more subbranches? The main branch will be the word that generates more subideas for you.

Obstacle #6—
Level of Detail

Detour #6—"How much detail should I put in my idea map?" How much information you include on your map primarily depends on the purpose. Once you have defined the specific purpose for the map, you must be sure that the level of detail is complete enough to meet that purpose, but is not crowded with information irrelevant to the task. Two people could create an idea map on the same subject and have completely different branch structures and amounts of detail. Familiarity with the material and how much you trust your memory will also impact the need for details.

Obstacle #7—
Looking for Perfection
on the First Draft

Detour #7—"I made a mistake and now I want to start over." Resist momentarily! Before doing anything ask the following questions:

1. Is it really critical to start over? Revisit the purpose of the idea map. Has it already served its purpose even though it may look messy? Are you being a perfectionist? Is redrawing a valuable use of your time?
2. Have you finished the majority of the idea map? If not, keep going until it is done. All possible changes can be handled in a second draft if necessary.

If you can consider this a draft, you are well organized for the next stage.

Once the idea map begins to take shape, it is easy to see where branches should move, where you could add pictures, and where certain ideas should have been ordered differently. That's one of the most useful things about an idea map. Sometimes conclusions or answers that weren't previously apparent will leap out at you. It is nearly impossible to make these observations while looking at pages of linear notes. What a great benefit! I usually consider my first attempt a draft—get all the ideas out, number the branches if there is a sequence, and then decide (based on my purpose) whether or not another draft is necessary.

For the perfectionists at heart—and you know who you are!—an idea map does not need to be a piece of artwork (although it can be). It is a tool—an organized holding tank of information to be used for a specific purpose. Once that purpose is fulfilled, there is no more need for the map unless there is a reason to keep it. As you begin to utilize the idea map for the purpose it was created for, you can write on it, cross things out, or throw it away!

There are still good reasons to reproduce and keep beautiful, final copies of idea maps. Here are a few:

- It will be distributed to others.
- It contains something you want to learn and put into long-term memory.
- It is a reference document like a strategic plan, a process, or a project.
- You are delivering a presentation from the idea map.

- It's a meeting agenda.
- To keep a history of your idea-mapping progress.
- Just because you want to!

Idea mapping is intended to save time and increase productivity; so when considering the need to start over, make wise decisions based on the purpose.

Obstacle #8—
Running Out of
Room & Paper

Detour #8—"I ran out of room around the central image. What do I do?" There are two easy solutions for this dilemma. One—get larger paper. That option is a good one to keep in mind for future idea maps, but is not helpful in the immediate situation. So grab a second sheet of paper. Use the same central image as before only make a note like "Page 2" somewhere within the central image. Off you go again!

A second option (if you know in advance that your map will contain a great amount of data) is not only to start with larger paper, but create a slightly larger central image. Now you have more room to attach your main branches.

This is an effective solution, especially when the issue is adding more branches, but what about adding more data to the branches. Now it is a function of running off the page. One idea is to draw an arrow off of the last branch(es) that fit on the page and write *Continued* on it. Flip the page over and continue mapping right at that spot. Alternatively, you can put another piece of paper next to the current one, keep mapping, and then tape them together when you are done. It might be ugly, but it works in a pinch!

Obstacle #9—
Images

Detour #9—"I can't remember what this picture meant." (We've already discussed the "I can't draw" syndrome in Chapter 4, which is a related and equally difficult obstacle.) In order to remember the meaning of pictures, I suggest starting with a combination of word and image. Implementing planned review periods of the idea map will also improve recall. (For more information on this, refer to the graphs on "Recall During Learning" and "Recall After Learning" in the book *Use Your Perfect Memory* by Tony Buzan.)

There is a temptation to have pictures randomly floating in the idea map. When this occurs, the association and meaning for floating images is difficult to remember, so keep pictures on a line and connected to a branch.

Often workshop participants draw a box or circle around the central image. There is no need to do this. Boxing in the central image creates a visual barrier between the central image and its main branches.

Here's a final note on images. If you are at the point of waving the white flag and saying, "I can't draw," consider this suggestion, which came from one of my first clients, an associate director in the financial industry. She became obsessed with collecting stickers she could use to represent the ideas in her maps in order to avoid drawing. Hey, whatever works!

Obstacle #10—
"Real-Time" Mapping

Detour #10—"I tried idea mapping a live 3-hour presentation. I couldn't figure out where the speaker was going and my map got messy. After 20 minutes I quit and returned to taking linear notes." I call this skill of mapping in the moment "real-time" idea mapping. It is an advanced skill and can take time and practice to become proficient. The person in the example above happened to get an unorganized presenter who had no outline or agenda to work from; the pace of information flow was quick; and his only exposure to idea mapping was from reading an article. He was a novice trying to slay a giant. See Chapter 13 for a full description on creating this type of map.

Obstacle #11—
The Idea Generation Process

Detour #11 covers an observation I see frequently from workshop participants. In the process of generating ideas for an idea map, I see people taking one of these ineffective approaches:

1. They identify all of their main branches before allowing themselves to move on to any detail levels.
2. They create one complete branch (including all its sub-branches, images, and details) before allowing themselves to add any other branches.

3. They are working on an application that has chronology (presentation, workflow, or other). They stop to think through each complete thought rather than letting the ideas bloom and flow simultaneously (capturing them as they come and placing them on the map where they best associate).

In each of these cases, thoughts are being forced onto the map unnaturally. This dilemma can be resolved by referring back to Lesson 2, which says "Where your brain goes, you will follow." By taking any of the previous approaches, the natural associative process is restricted. As a thought comes to mind—it goes on the paper. Just ask the question, "Where does this thought fit?" You may decide to move things around later, but for now capture the ideas as they come. It might be a good idea to have a *miscellaneous* branch as speed is the focus here. You can organize them later if appropriate.

Working through these obstacles is all part of the learning process. Be patient and persistent. A lifetime of linear note taking may compete a bit with your learning until idea mapping is an equally strong habit. Practice mapping frequently to improve your skills and make it a tool you can use naturally. My hope is that this tool will be fun and incredibly beneficial. See the idea map in Figure 5.8 for a summary of this chapter.

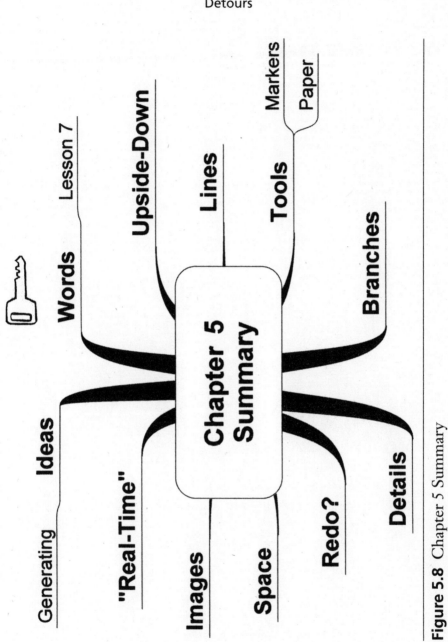

Figure 5.8 Chapter 5 Summary

6

Applications

Now you know how to idea map, have created several examples, and understand the laws. This chapter will cover the following topics:

- Learning about the value of seeing other people's maps
- Viewing idea maps created by 11 professionals from around the world

Learning By Seeing

For many people there is a big gap between knowing how to idea map and actually applying it to something worthwhile. Seeing others' models will act as the bridge. These examples will open your eyes to a wealth of possible uses and will help spark creative applications of your own.

Having spent nearly 15 years teaching idea mapping to thousands of people, I have been exposed to an amazing variety of applications. Seeing how and understanding why others have been successful with this tool is an excellent way to learn how to incorporate idea mapping into your work and life. In this chapter, I will highlight hand-drawn examples from business people around the globe. These maps will follow the laws closely. Each will have a different use, level of complexity, style, and purpose. The selections will be a mix of typical and uncommon business applications. Following will be a series of application descriptions, benefits, and the associated idea maps. Enjoy meeting some of my friends. (The idea maps that are too large for this book and color versions of all maps are available at www.IdeaMappingSuccess .com.)

Lesson Eight— Get ideas for idea-mapping applications by seeing others' examples.

Data Collection for Annual Job Review

Anyone who has ever had a job has been through the review process. Many dread the thought of preparing for their review as they painfully attempt to recall and describe all the important data for an entire year. Without good records, some accomplishments are already distant memories. Jared Kelner had a better idea.

He is a service account manager for a large internet hardware manufacturer. He is responsible for selling the appropriate services from his company's services portfolio to one of America's largest communications companies. Some of the services he sells are proactive engineering services, professional installation and project management services, and maintenance/technical support services. Once the new services are in place, he works with an extended team to ensure the services are delivered with the highest level of quality and accuracy, and that services are constantly exceeding the customers' expectations.

Kelner states, "It becomes cumbersome and challenging at times to ensure that you discuss all of the year's key topics during the review. When you have multiple spreadsheets and word documents to sort through, there is a greater chance of missing some critical information. I created this idea map to keep a running log of my annual activities at work so that when it comes time to sit down with my manager for my annual review, I will be able to quickly and efficiently present a summary of everything I did in the past year. By consolidating everything on to one idea map, the discussion becomes very fluid, natural, and comprehensive. In general, the benefit [of] idea mapping this topic for my annual review [is that it] helps to focus the conversation during the review itself. Prior to creating this idea map, I used a spreadsheet as my information repository. My intention is to add content to the map at the end of each week. Ultimately, I can use the information on the idea map as my benchmark for setting the next year's goals and objectives."

Figure 6.1 is Kelner's initial template to which he will add data throughout the year. He has six main branches, each representing large amounts of data. They are *Financial Goals*, *Meetings*, *Conflicts*, *Training*, *Travel/Expense*, and *Major Wins*. An image—rather than a word—describes each branch. The map will be explained by using the clock positions.

One o'clock Branch—Financial Goals

At the one o'clock position are his financial goals showing year-to-date progress toward annual sales goals. Kelner mentions, "By posting this information on my wall, it is a constant reminder of what I have ahead of me in terms of sales objectives."

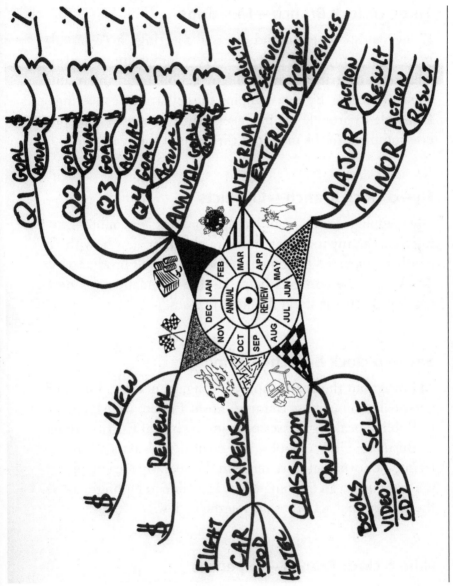

Figure 6.1 Data Collection for Annual Job Review

Three o'clock Branch—Meetings

Kelner adds, "Internal and external meetings make up almost 50% of my time. It becomes very important to continually track the participants, content, action items, and results of each meeting. By idea mapping the key strategic meetings, I am able to provide my manager [with] a detailed, yet concise summary of the meetings throughout the year."

Five o'clock Branch—Conflicts

"By mapping the major and minor conflicts I encounter during the year, my manager and I are able to review how these conflicts impacted the business and my overall productivity. Tracking these conflicts helps lay the foundation for next year's projects for streamlining processes."

Seven o'clock Branch—Training

"Throughout the year, employees engage in many forms of personal and business training. From Project Management to Public Speaking classes or from Technical Certifications to Business Theory books, it is critical to discuss all of the training efforts that were made in the year. By idea mapping the training on an ongoing basis, I am able to highlight all of the educational activities during the review."

Nine o'clock Branch—Expenses

"Measuring, tracking, and managing your business expense report is critical to the financial success of the company. By mapping the ongoing expenses throughout the year, I am able to provide a detailed summary of all monies issued for things like airplane fares, hotel and rental car charges, and meals."

Eleven o'clock Branch—Major Wins

"The branch of major wins is a critical part of the annual review process. It is very important to highlight my significant accomplishments in order to help position a promotion, a bonus, or a special assignment. By mapping the major wins throughout the year, the discussion around this point becomes extremely effective."

In Kelner's example, he was preparing for his own review. I know leaders who create similar idea maps when preparing to give reviews to their employees. Whether on the giving or receiving end, make an idea map for your next review!

Estate Planning

Liza Seiner is a lawyer who uses idea maps for her clients who need estate-planning services. When I met Liza in October of 2004, the beauty and artistry of her maps overwhelmed me. I was even more surprised to discover she was a lawyer. She did not fit my stereotype. Idea mapping renurtured her love of drawing and in addition provided a practical reason to use them with clients. (See Figure 6.2 for Liza's Estate Planning Map.) She now combines her ability to teach idea mapping with her legal background. Refer to Figure 6.2 as you read her description of this map.

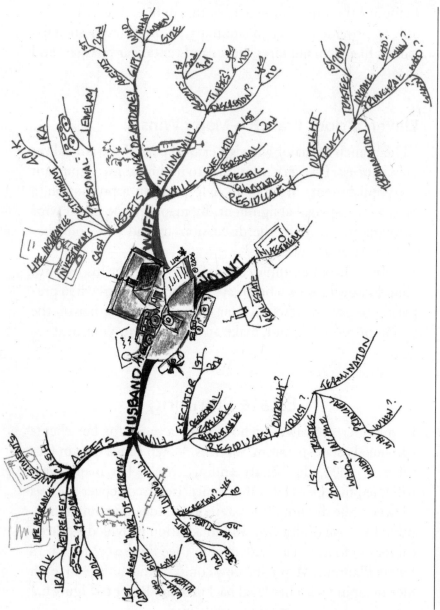

Figure 6.2 Estate Planning

I began using the maps in my client meetings when I realized that they helped me to organize my own thinking. The first ones that I used were for clients that were coming to see me after several years. They had done estate-planning work (meaning that they had created Wills, Powers of Attorney for finances, and Living Wills for healthcare decisions). I needed to refresh my memory on the various terms we had chosen to include in their documents. Doing an idea map was a review and preparation tool.

When I got to the actual meeting, I used the idea maps as an "agenda" to review with them what we had done in the past. Normally, I can expect to spend about 1½ hours in a meeting with a client (whether it's a new client or a review). By using the maps for review, we were easily able to save thirty minutes, and they were very appreciative of the review. It made their understanding much greater, and we could write the changes they wanted to make on the map.

With new clients, much of the information that I present to them has to do with explaining how the documents work to achieve their goals. The explanations are still necessary, but the visual layout allows them to grasp the material better, and I think they give better responses to questions that I have about their goals and desires.

Every client that I have seen using an idea map has expressed their enjoyment of the process. The following gives a little perspective on the size and complexity of cases with which they have been used: I have used them with clients that had very few assets, but perhaps "unconventional" family structures (i.e., no children, but many people they wished to provide for at their deaths); large asset clients (one in particular had multiple businesses, complex inheritance issues, and unfocused goals); and the "average" couple, with kids and grandchildren, who wanted to provide for their families, and make sure that decisions about finances and healthcare were taken care of so they didn't have to worry about it.

The map in Figure 6.2 is the template Liza uses to gather client information, understand the goals, and finally meet with the client.

Decision—To Move or Not to Move?

Vanda North is currently the founder and director of The Learning Consortium, a global training organization based out of the United Kingdom that specializes in accelerated learning techniques for increased business productivity and profits. Vanda has over 30 years of experience working with world business leaders. She founded The Buzan Centres and was the global director of the Buzan Organization from 1988 to 2006. Figure 6.3 shows Vanda's idea map, which captures the critical issues around a decision to relocate their headquarters.

I was aware for some time that I might need to move my offices from Bournemouth, U.K., to another location. At the time the decision wasn't pressing; however, if things continued as they were, it would become more necessary. After considering many points, there still wasn't a clear-cut direction. I began to explore the issues in more detail.

There was another aspect—the feelings of the rest of the

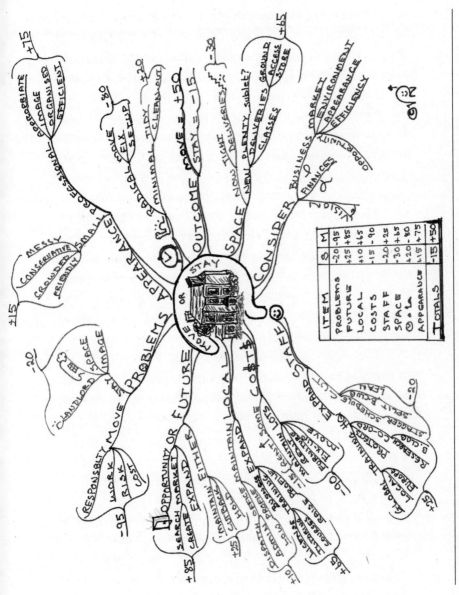

Figure 6.3 Decision

team. I wanted to find out how a move would affect them. We had a team meeting and BrainBloomed ™ the main considerations (red) while creating an idea map. Then we used a color code for either staying (green) or moving (purple). Each person completed a color copy of the map with any issues about that topic and gave a rating (or weighting) to each branch. The scale went from −100 (negative impact) to +100 (positive impact). Everyone added their own thoughts, worries, concerns, hopes, and the specific impact it would have on them. It was a great chance to really know how each person felt.

There were several surprises and some very valuable input that may well not have come to light if this process had not been conducted. Further, even if people were negative about the situation, they felt better for the chance to have voiced their opinions and to have them recorded and validated. I collated all of the input and computed an overall score to determine a suggested direction.

The map consolidated ideas from the powerful brains throughout the entire organization. Further, everyone really felt that they contributed and had assisted in a big decision. Regardless of the decision, some people would not be happy— at least that was now known. It was therefore an easy matter to discuss alternatives (given the circumstances). In most cases, the person had a solution for their own problem, and that made them feel good as well.

I would not make a decision based only on this process; however, to involve the whole team and to have a strong awareness for how the people that make things happen on a daily basis feel and what can be done, I think it is the best and easiest way to move forward.

The end of the story was that we did decide to move. It was one of the best decisions we have made, and everyone felt good about it.

Vision/Mission

It is a well-known fact that creating a written vision for life and work significantly increases the likelihood of achieving that vision. Yet, how many of us take the time and effort to do this? Figure 6.4 is the most significant idea map I have ever created for my work and life.

I mentioned earlier that I taught Covey's *Seven Habits of Highly Effective Leaders* while working for a previous employer. During this workshop, each participant does some soul-searching exercises to lay the groundwork for writing a mission statement. Various experts want to distinguish a vision from a mission. I'm not going to get hung up on the semantics. Call it what you want! The basic idea is to create a vision of you and your life as you want to see it lived out both personally and professionally. It typically will not change although life circumstances change.

During the Covey workshop participants create a draft of their vision and are encouraged to finish it after class. Over a 9-month period while teaching this class, my guilt steadily increased because I had never completed my own vision and felt like a hypocrite telling others to do something I had not. I had completed all the exercises, but could not seem to put something as important as my entire life into a nice paragraph, a list of bullets, or any of the other recommended formats.

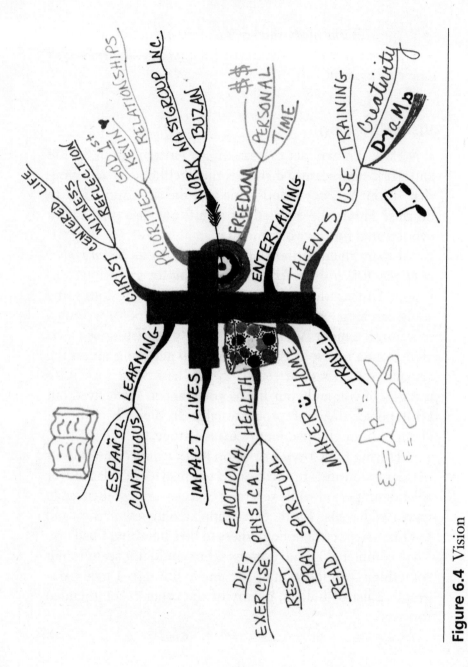

Figure 6.4 Vision

I was home recovering from some minor surgery one day and had one of those "aha!" moments. It's actually a bit embarrassing to admit that although I had been idea mapping for 5 years by now, it never dawned on me to try putting my vision in that format. I immediately located the exercises from the class, all of the preparation, and my weak attempt at a draft. Within 30 minutes I completely converted this painful linear document into an idea map. That was in February of 1997. Since then I've only made one tiny revision. I reduced it to a 6″ × 3.5″ page and had it laminated. I have a small binder that contains my PDA, some unlined paper, and a four-color pen. In the front of the binder is now this reduced version of my vision map. It was easy to create, and now it helps me to make better decisions and shapes how and where I spend my time.

The idea map itself is self-explanatory. The icons in the central image hold volumes of words for me, so the use of imagery saved what would have been pages of linear descriptions. My main branches cover work, life, learning, using my talents, freedom, things I enjoy, and my spiritual commitment. It has stood the test of time and has been a great reminder for me and a source of inspiration.

Vision—Getting Started

This is an activity and an idea map that ties to the previous vision application. It is so important for individuals to have a vision for their lives and careers. I've occasionally asked people to map their vision as a workshop activity, and it is frequently highlighted as one of the most beneficial aspects

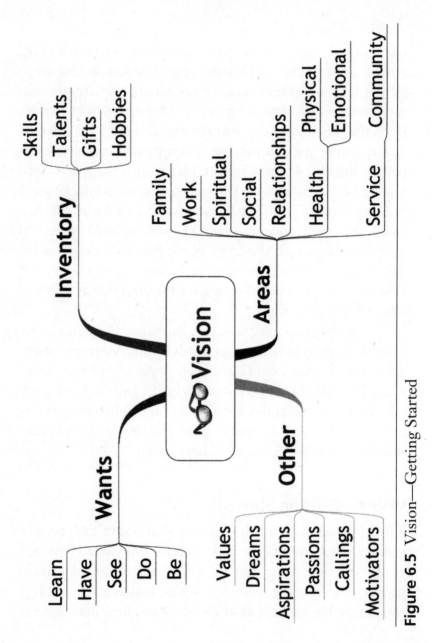

Figure 6.5 Vision—Getting Started

of the course. Therefore, I'm going to strongly encourage the creation of this kind of idea map. Your map will have branches that are different from my example in Figure 6.4 and a different amount of detail. Here are a few suggestions as you begin this activity.

As a starting point, I've created an idea map (refer to Figure 6.5) that provides some categories to foster the thinking process around your own vision. I use this same map for workshop participants and project it on a screen throughout this part of the course. (It was created using software, and we'll get to that in the next chapter.) It's always good to start by taking an inventory of your strengths and talents—both used and unused. What relationships and areas of life are important to you? What provides meaning in your life? What do you want to accomplish? What would you do for free if money was no issue? What do you hope to be? Do you feel your work and life have purpose? What provides that purpose (or would provide it if it is missing)? What is it that really matters in life? These are just some questions to get you started. Don't limit yourself to this map. Use it to spark additional thoughts about your own life.

As you consider the major areas of your life vision, begin an idea map. Capture all of your ideas without editing right now. Then leave it alone for a day or even a week. Repeat this process several times without looking back at previous maps. Then sit down with all your maps. Consolidate a final (final for now at least) idea map of everything that seems important at this stage. You may find you leave some things out, or you may find a new way to capture multiple thoughts into one word or image. This process may take some time, so allow yourself several drafts if necessary. Add, change, and delete branches from this map until you feel it is finished. The final product will be worth the effort.

This is an added note for those in leadership positions. In his book *Primal Leadership*, Daniel Goleman talks about the importance of individual and organizational vision. For leaders managing a team of employees, have each team member create a vision map for his or her work and life. Then help him or her live out the part of that vision that can be realized in the workplace. Use the Team Mapping Method described in Chapter 9 to create a vision for your organization. You will have a happier and more committed team. Objectives will be clearer, and there will be a reduction in the wasted time that is caused by confusion around purpose. Others will be fighting to get onto your team! The results will amaze you!

Problem Employee and Difficult Discussion

Karen Maggard was the second vice president for the sales division of a large insurance company. She was having a serious problem with one of her employees. As she described the various issues over the phone, I mapped out her concerns and then faxed her the map. It was a helpful tool going into her next round of discussions with this employee. The map kept her focus on the issues and not the emotions of the situation. See Figure 6.6.

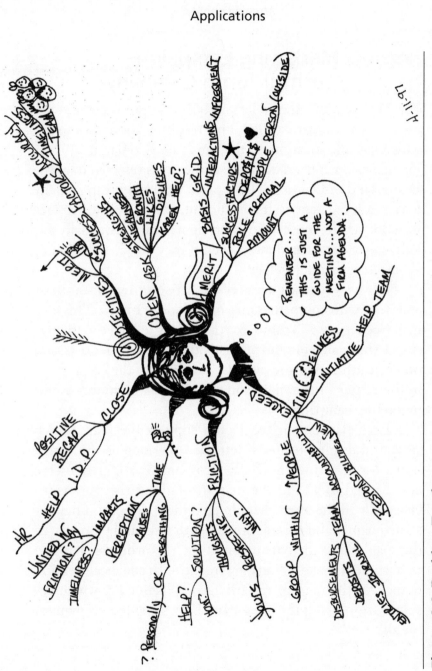

Figure 6.6 Problem Employee

Marketing Campaign—
Youthful Tooth Company

For 25 years, Jeff Alexander has been the president and co-owner of a company called The Youthful Tooth Company, which has four locations in the San Francisco Bay area. During television appearances, the company is referred to as the Disneyland of Dentistry. It's a place where kids can actually have fun at the dentist. It is a colorful, fun, and exciting place to work where those who need dental care (especially for kids) never get turned away, even if they are financially unable to care for themselves.

Jeff uses his vast areas of expertise to teach seminars and work with companies on a multitude of topics. This idea map (see Figure 6.7) came from a seminar Jeff gave in the Bay Area to his managers and other visiting doctors, dentists, and other health care professionals. The logo of the company is in the center of the map, and the seminar topic was a new marketing campaign.

Each participant received a copy of the map, which served multiple purposes. Jeff used the map as the actual notes for teaching the 2-day program. Participants were encouraged to add to the map throughout the seminar—especially in the areas that affected them directly. They assigned names and completion dates to tasks and then posted the map where their team could see the progress. Jeff had each student make a "fun agreement"—to add a celebration branch to the map to reward accomplishments, which resulted from using the idea map. This provided enjoyment for all!

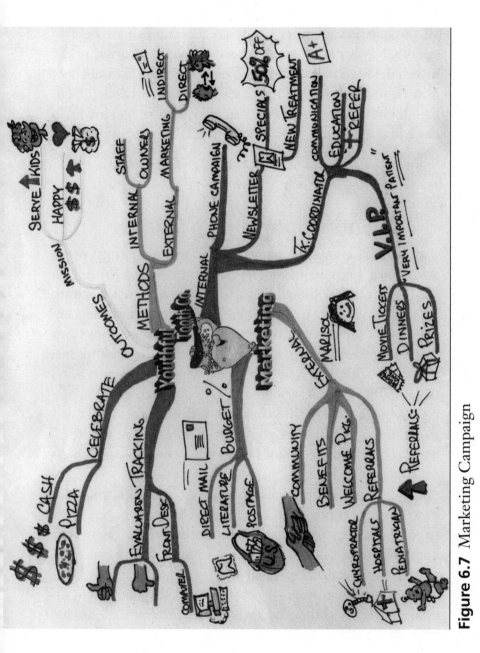

Figure 6.7 Marketing Campaign

When Jeff delivers seminars for companies, he frequently leaves them a copy of his idea map as a review of the material. He recommends that they enlarge the map and post it in a common area for all the staff to constantly see (like in the lunchroom, but out of view of customers or patients). He has had great results with this method. The map acts as not only a reminder, but also shows progress and evaluation on unfinished projects.

Entire Books—(Big Maps!)

Pete Wilkins is a senior manager with the Consulting Group at Deloitte. In May of 2005, he attended a 5-day QBI (Qualified Buzan Instructor) certification workshop I was teaching in Vancouver, British Columbia. In preparation for the certification, candidates were required to map three books and then bring their maps to class. This is a daunting task for beginners. Candidates used their own discretion to determine the amount of detail in their maps. I suggested they include enough data to learn the concepts and skills they will need to teach others. They usually create their maps on $11'' \times 17''$ paper. For the larger books, I recommend one map per chapter. Then I met Pete.

When it was time for the group to review his prework, Pete unrolled three LARGE pieces of flipchart paper. Each page was a map that captured an entire book. They were huge, beautifully done, had many images, and contained a high level of detail. Pete was able to learn and internalize volumes of information through this activity. He put them up on the wall in his home for a while after the course. This enabled him to review the material frequently and have greater recall of the information. Figure 6.8 will show you a photograph of one of his giant maps! This is an idea map of the book *Get Ahead* by Vanda North. See www.IdeaMapping Success.com for Pete's other two large book idea maps.

Dual Core

Gregg Stokes is a partner and executive art director for Clarity Creative Group in Las Vegas, Nevada. Refer to Figure 6.9 as he describes his application.

>*Idea maps serve as a detailed visual reference to capture large quantities of information. At a glance, I can get a project overview and see the overall project structure. Also present is the ability to see details that are included in the branching.*
>
>*This project was a 3D animation based around several scenarios. I created this Dual Core idea map to show relationships and continuity between scenarios. At the core of the project was a new microprocessor architecture—which is a highly technical product. The many benefits that the end user derives from this advanced technology were established as the deliverable.*
>
>*The outcome was clarity. After many meetings and discussions, I provided a map that distilled hours of discussions, hours of conversation, and pages of notes into one map. The project was given the green light, and we proceeded to a full-blown 3D animation.*
>
>*The animation served as a vehicle that brought an awareness to the internal sales force on how this new technology*

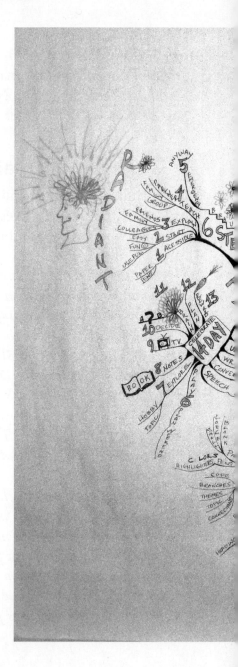

Figure 6.8 Get Ahead

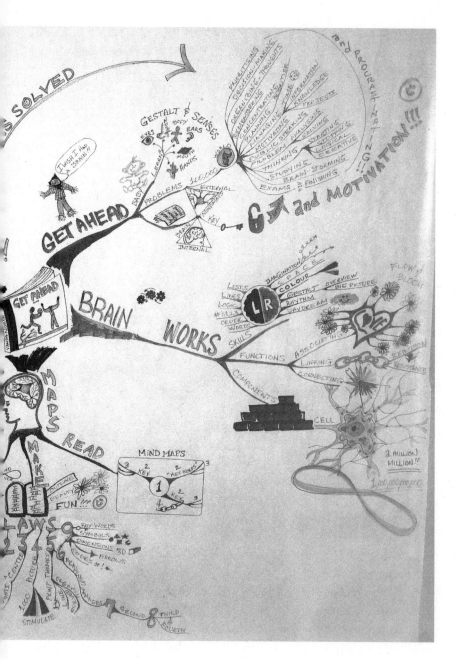

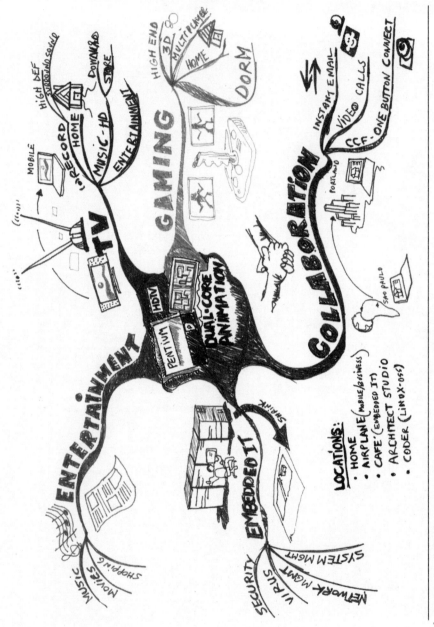

Figure 6.9 Dual Core

should be explained to their customers. It also created excitement as it was used to close a very technical presentation that needed a flashy ending.

I have used idea maps countless times to summarize technical details for projects that need to be organized and structured. I have always received positive feedback from my clients as to how the idea map was the first time they saw the project as a structured whole—instead of pieces and parts.

Cancer Map

Although the focus of this book is the business applications of idea mapping, we all know that it is virtually impossible to separate our professional lives from our personal. I met Judy Grewell on February 8, 1996. In all my idea-mapping experiences, this is one of the most profound and unique idea maps I have ever been privileged to see. I'll let Judy tell the following story in her own words. Refer to Figure 6.10.

This idea map was done by my late husband, John, and me during the last few weeks of his life. I had taken a class, taught by Jamie Nast, on February 8, 1996. John and I began the idea map on February 9, 1996, continuing it energetically until a day or two before his death on March 18, 1996. (I finished some details of it afterward.) We had so many things to sort out and think about regarding his cancer treatment and other decisions once he was determined to be terminally ill on February 28, 1996. Using the idea-mapping strategy, we were able to organize the immense array of details during this stressful time. We put a large piece of chart paper on the wall

Figure 6.10 Cancer Map

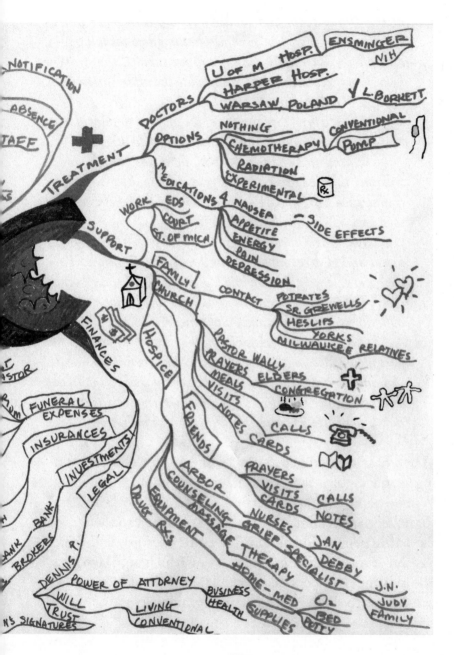

in the dining room and captured thoughts together nearly every night. Even when John was finding deep thinking very difficult (he eventually died of a brain tumor), the strategy helped him see, understand, and add to the information until a couple of days before his death.

Here is a brief explanation of the map; in the actual map there are boxes around major points of consideration.

Treatment is the first branch. John was already under treatment for the cancer, but since it was rapidly progressing, the question was could we do more? The subbranches were doctors, options, and medications.

Next was Support. These branches were the sources of moral and physical support to us during John's illness. They were work, family, church, and Hospice. The following branch covered both financial and legal matters such as John's living will, investments, insurance, and funeral expenses.

This last branch (Final Planning) was the most difficult part of the idea map, since this occurred when John's death was imminent (within days); he did as much of this with me as he was able. It included the funeral, cemetery, obituary, thank you notes, my leave of absence, and notifications.

When Judy created her idea map, she was a technical training manager of a large information technology company. When she attended the second day of the workshop and shared her application, it was a very sobering experience for the entire group. Thankfully, the story does not end there. Several years later, she married a wonderful man, Dave Bess. She continues to be a dear friend, and I thank her for her willingness to share such a personal example.

An Introduction to Leadership Coaching

Kirsty Hayes is the founder of The Learning Attitude, an organizational and leadership development company specializing in improving personal and organizational performance. She is based out of Sydney, Australia, has over 22 years experience in commerce, and is an accomplished international keynote speaker. She is the author of *Leadership Coaching: A Practical Guide* published by Pearson Education Australia, and the author of *Dancing With Brilliance*. Here is Kirsty's description of her idea map (see Figure 6.11):

> *This idea map summarizes the introduction chapter of my book* Leadership Coaching—A Practical Guide. *It outlines what coaching is, the benefits of coaching, why coach, and how to get the most out of this book. Each chapter in this book is summarized with an idea map. Prior to writing this book, I created a mega map outlining all the content I wanted to cover and the order it was to be covered. I drafted the text from the mega map. This map was recreated from my original map as a subset of the entire book.*

Company Mission Statement

Gan F. Tong is a partner in a company called MindeXtension in Milan, Italy. Gan has years of experience in high-level corporate leadership and business. She is a consultant, corporate business trainer, and certified trainer for Franklin Covey courses. I met Gan and Dario Biondo, the founder of their

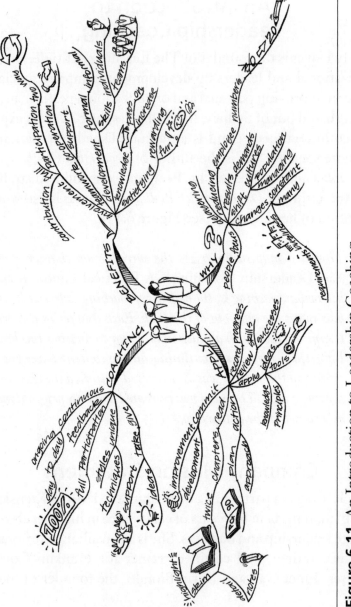

Figure 6.11 An Introduction to Leadership Coaching

company, in March of 2005 when I certified them both as idea-mapping instructors. They are a brilliant team, and what follows is an example of how they work together to bring excellence to their clients. Gan describes her map (see Figure 6.12) as follows:

> *I did this map in about 15 minutes after reading loads of articles and books on how to write powerful mission statements for companies. In order to capture all the ideas that I liked from those materials, I summarized them into a quick idea map.*
>
> *Dario then used this map to conduct a brainstorming exercise (see the reference to BrainBloom™ in Chapter 9) for a group of four business owners of a mid-size electronics wholesale distributor in Tuscany, Italy. Their company is the market leader in that region.*
>
> *The idea map helped Dario to walk them through a very time consuming and difficult exercise without any problem. After spending a day with these business owners and going through the various stages of the exercise, Dario gave them a week or so to work on their own and complete these statements. The outcome was that they completed their company mission statement from those exercises and included the statement in their new brochure.*

So you can see from the examples throughout this chapter what a valuable tool idea mapping can be to help collect, sort, clarify, consolidate, and present large amounts of information—whether personal or professional, whether in stressful times or not, whether making decisions, developing marketing plans, or creating a vision. See Figure 6.13 for a sum-

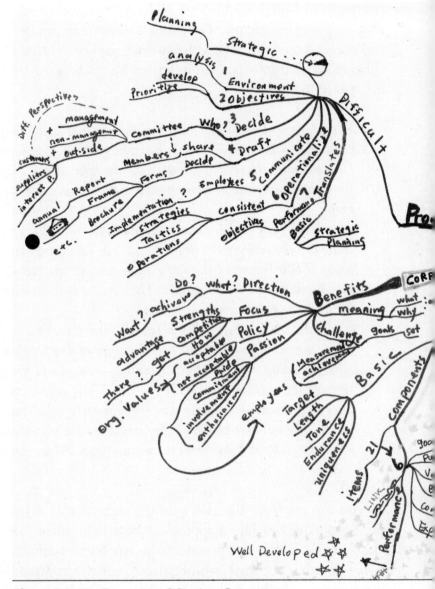

Figure 6.12 Company Mission Statement

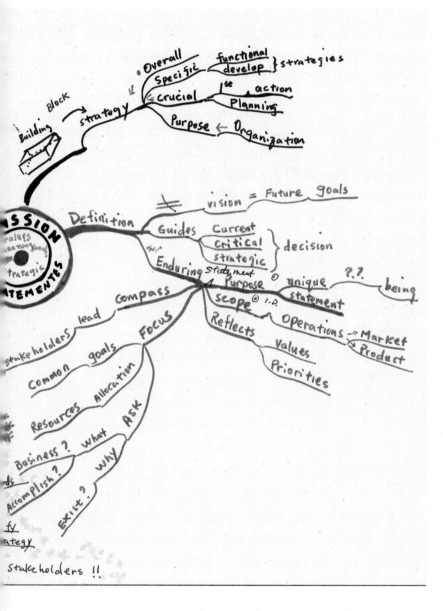

mary of all the different uses for idea maps discussed in this chapter. Idea maps assist people with their planning and organizing. They give you a whole picture of the issue at hand rather than scattered pieces.

Now that you have read these stories and seen the associated maps, create an idea map that will assist you in life or business. Continue to work on a map for your work and life vision. In the next chapter, I will introduce an amazing software package that will become a necessary tool as you become a more proficient user of idea mapping.

Figure 6.13 Chapter 6 Summary

CHAPTER

7

The Question of Software

n nearly every workshop I teach someone asks, "Is there any software for idea mapping?" Of course, the answer is yes. This chapter will:

- Offer some criteria for choosing software
- Discuss the benefits of software over hand-drawn maps
- Address some concerns about using software
- Spotlight a number of applications developed using the Mindjet MindManager Pro 6 product
- Suggest some activities using a trial version of software

Software Criteria

I have seen and used many varieties of idea-mapping software. When considering a software purchase, keep the following things in mind for your final decision:

- Stability of the product and company
- Pricing/Budget
- Seamless integration with other products
- Features
- Customer support availability and responsiveness
- Number of preloaded images and icons
- Your purpose, needs, and applications
- The volume and complexity of the data you need to manage

- MAC or Windows compatibility
- Products available that extend the use of that software

Nearly every company enables you to download a trial version of its product so that you can play with and test the software for yourself prior to any purchase. Before making a decision, try a few products based on your criteria. I own several packages in order to be well acquainted with a variety of top products, but when it comes to actually using software—I am a Mindjet gal. (See www.mindjet.com for more information.) They are top leaders in their industry, are endorsed by *The Wall Street Journal* (September 2002), and meet all of my application criteria and then some. Mindjet has a large group of partners who develop add-in software products that make this particular mapping tool even more useful. The idea maps shown in this book were created using the Mindjet MindManager Pro 6 product. Keep in mind the need to choose a product that is best for you.

Benefits of Using Software

I'm not saying you should use software for all of your idea maps. It's not always convenient to carry a laptop. However, using software has some major advantages. Below are some of the benefits to consider.

Ease of Revisions

After (or even during) the creation of a hand-drawn map, it is common to sit back, take a holistic view, and see a need to reorganize your ideas. This is both good and bad. The good news is that the idea map provides the vehicle to see better connections and associations between thoughts and to make corrections. The bad news is that if you need a polished version of the map or want to continue adding to the branches, starting over by hand is time consuming. The software quickly and easily enables the user to move branches or sub-branches anywhere with a simple "click and drag."

Removes the Fear of Drawing Images

There are people who enjoy and appreciate the value of images, but don't want to put the time into learning how to draw. Some even have emotional scars from childhood caused by their lack of artistic talent. Mindjet's database of images, symbols, and icons solves this problem.

Managing Large Volumes of Data

Here's where you can begin to see massive time savings and refined thinking processes. Managing data is different from collecting data. Managing information requires doing something with the knowledge gathered in your map. With Mindjet you have the option of exporting this data into Power-Point, Project, Outlook, or Word. There can be hyperlinks within the branches of the map that link directly to other documents, websites, or idea maps.

Increasingly, people are using electronic maps not just to capture ideas and information, but as an efficient way to visualize and act on data. MindManager, for example, integrates with salesforce.com, enabling sales professionals to see (in one map) information collected from more than 30 separate salesforce.com screens. The map format also enables the sales reps and their managers to generate strategies to close sales faster. This ability to gain a clear overview—and then to conduct thinking and planning around that overview, provides a key competitive advantage for people using idea maps.

Presentations

Some people use maps as visual aids during their presentations. You could use a hand-drawn example if you wanted; however, if the audience and subject matter require a cleaner look, creating your map using the software is an easy solution. As mentioned previously, the software enables you to plan your presentation using the map format, and then simply export it to Microsoft PowerPoint to create the actual slide deck.

Software Concerns

Occasionally, a few people hesitate when I mention using software to create idea maps. I have to admit—that was my first reaction many years ago. I would rate myself as mildly computer literate, and I believe I was intimidated by the thought of putting down the markers and learning something outside my comfort zone. That was before I experienced how easy it was to use the software. Now I could not function without it.

There are even more individuals who have been introduced to idea mapping through the use of Mindjet's products who can't imagine ever drawing maps by hand! I don't want to sweep potential software concerns under the rug, so let me address those issues before we move on.

Hand-Drawn Maps are More Memorable

According to memory research, the more senses (seeing, hearing, touching, tasting, and smelling) we use when learning—the greater the recall. (See Chapter One of *Memory Power* by Scott Hagwood.) Therefore, the kinesthetic aspect of actually drawing the map may add connections and associations that would enhance recall. This might be a valid argument if remembering is your primary purpose.

Loss of Flexibility

Getting the computer to duplicate what you can create by hand is sometimes challenging. Let's face it—the computer is a great tool, but it is still not the same as drawing. I could also argue that the software actually provides more flexibility by utilizing the electronic format. Now you can import information into the map, email the map (or only a portion of the map), or export the map to a variety of other software products.

Takes More Time

Some have said that they spend more time playing with the software to get just the right look. Whether it is formatting branches or searching for the right color, it can become time consuming. It's that perfectionist at work again! Sometimes the desired image doesn't exist within the software database, so off you go to the internet (for an undetermined amount of time) to hopefully find it. Keep in mind that some of this is part of the learning curve. I have found that once people get used to the software, this argument disappears. Plus, you can create templates with all your favorite settings.

Summary of Benefits and Concerns

Despite my initial reaction, I very quickly became an avid user of both hand-drawn and software-generated idea maps. There is no reason to argue that one method is better than another, because it is an individual choice and both provide an excellent forum for capturing ideas. The bottom line is this: There are people who prefer software, some who prefer drawing their maps by hand, and the majority of people use both depending on their individual purpose. I encourage you to find one software product so that you have the flexibility to use it based on the application. You will be the judge.

Lesson Nine—
Try using software.

Mindjet Software Applications

The rest of this chapter is devoted to sharing a variety of stories and applications from business people around the globe. These maps will follow the laws closely. (The maps that are too large for this book and color versions of all maps are available at www.IdeaMappingSuccess.com.)

Strategic Marketing

Terry Moore, president of Terry Moore & Associates, Incorporated, provides consulting services for companies around the world. His organization specializes in strategic marketing. Terry is an expert user and facilitator of idea mapping. What follows is his answer to a conceptual dilemma. The idea map he refers to is Figure 7.1.

Research is often the heart of a consulting assignment, and there is frequently a wealth of data to be mined and analyzed. The choice of analytical tools can be critical to timely success.

Often the data are quantitative. When confronted by a large amount of quantitative data, there are many statistical tools available to the analyst—sampling techniques, multiple-regression, coincidence correlation, exponential smoothing, and others. Most of these tools use computers to parse and refine the raw data, which yields some sort of processed information: graphs, intercepts, or statistical measures.

Frequently our work involves large amounts of qualitative information: cultural information, customer behavior patterns, consumer-product interactions, et cetera. Each of these may involve thousands of qualitative data points. What does one do with a large amount of qualitative information? How does one begin to organize and analyze it so that one may make sense of the common realities underlying the raw data?

Too often analysts assign some sort of numerical system to the data and then use one of the statistical techniques to analyze it. That is usually not very satisfactory. What one needs is a way to conceptualize a large amount of information so

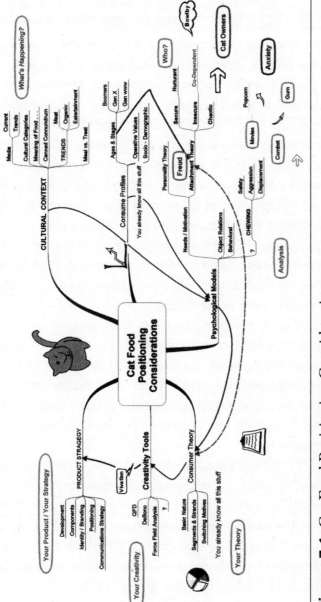

Figure 7.1 Cat Food Positioning Considerations

that one can "get one's mind around it" in order to understand it and be able to draw conclusions.

Idea mapping offers the power to represent qualitative data, describe relationships, and enable one to see the "big picture." Further, mapping allows us to represent data in a way that facilitates the conceptualizing of its meaning. It provides a "map," which makes it possible to observe macrophenomena, discover trends, and generate creative options. Idea mapping makes it possible to represent multiple dimensions of a situation without losing sight of any of its parts; it is an efficient way to manage an overwhelming amount of qualitative information. Finally, it offers a way to present information to clients in a graphic form that is both easy to understand and data rich. Often, an entire strategic plan can be represented in one map. This greatly assists in communicating our work to our clients.

The other major part of our work involves the development of complex conceptual systems for analyzing markets, product development, consumer behavior, and other complicated phenomena. The ability to conceptualize and understand these things is key to being able to succeed with a certain market, product, and customer. Here is one example [refer to Figure 7.1]:

Our challenge was to create a process for developing a product-positioning strategy for a major pet food manufacturer. The objective was to design a process for the development of a strategy that incorporated an analysis of consumer culture with all the useful theories of consumer behavior and then draw on the correct set of creative resources to produce a positioning strategy for a new line of cat food.

This map describes the necessary elements in the development of the plan. Starting at the top right branch and moving clockwise:

1. *Market variables. The details of the cultural context in which the market operates.*
2. *Consumer profiles.*
3. *Conceptual systems for understanding consumer behavior: needs/motivation, attachment theory, psychoanalytic theory, et cetera.*
4. *Consumer theory. Behavior of consumer groups. Branding and segmentation.*
5. *Creative applications, which can be brought to bear on the development of product positioning.*
6. *Product strategies, which will incorporate all of the above.*

In the final step of the process, all the common business strategic components are utilized (branding, communications strategy, etc.), but only after all the environmental, psychological, demographic, and consumer factors are taken into consideration.

Training/Learning Event

You met Vanda North, founder and director of The Learning Consortium, in Chapter 6 with her description of a decision map. This time she used Mindjet software to create an idea map for a different application. (See Figure 7.2.)

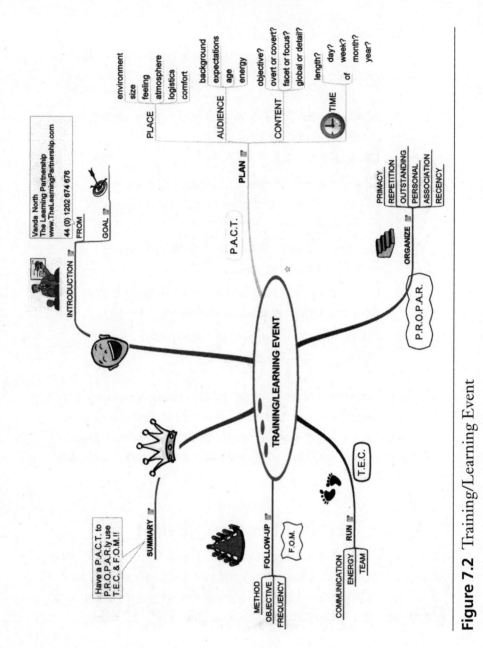

Figure 7.2 Training/Learning Event

A training magazine contacted Vanda to write an article on how to plan for a training event. Her submission deadline was very tight. She used the Mindjet software to outline her immediate ideas, and reorganized the sequence of the branches later. She used a feature of the software that provides space for writing text notes that link to the associated branch. Here she wrote the linear content of the article and added pictures to spark creative thinking. When Vanda finished the map, all she had to do was consolidate the text notes, convert it into a MS Word document, and it was done! She completed the entire article in the same amount of time she expected it would take to finish only a draft of the outline.

Not only was the article received favorably, but this event map has become a wonderful template to use when planning a meeting, conference, or workshop. When printed, this map comes with all the text notes. Users can add comments for their specific plans, links to documents that need copying, spreadsheets for budgeting purposes, websites for research, and the Power Point slides for the presentation during the event. The entire event is available in one map.

Sales Cycle

Dr. Andrei Jablokow earned a doctorate in engineering, taught mechanical engineering at Pennsylvania State University and Drexel University, and has 15 years of information technology (IT) sales experience. Andrei shares a series of three idea maps that will take you from an initial approach to a corporate client, to an initial conversation with a prospect, and finally to an IT project presentation.

Cold Call

Refer to Figure 7.3. This idea map is an example of a script for approaching a prospect for the first time via telephone. Usually when you call someone you are interrupting them, and they do not have time to talk at that moment. I use this initial approach to schedule a follow-up telephone conversation for a date and time that is convenient for them to talk.

Having the script represented as a map (and having it in front of you when you call) enables you to stay on track with your intention as well as respond appropriately based upon what happens during the call—prospect answers, you get the administrative assistant, you get the wrong person, or you get voicemail, etc.

Initial Call

Refer to Figure 7.4. This idea map is an example of a script for an initial 15–20 minute scheduled conversation on the phone. You can use this map to guide the conversation through a series of questions as well as briefly present why the prospect should continue their conversation with you. The intention of this call is to mutually decide if a face-to-face meeting would be appropriate. You do not need to cover everything on the map to be effective. If you and the prospect decide to meet, the rest of the information can be covered at that time. Developing an idea map for your purposes enables you to plan for any question the prospect may ask.

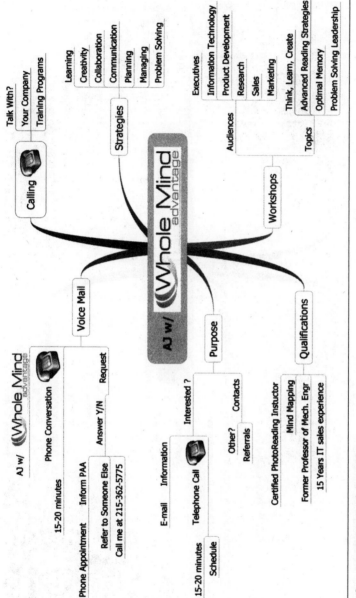

Figure 7.3 Cold Call

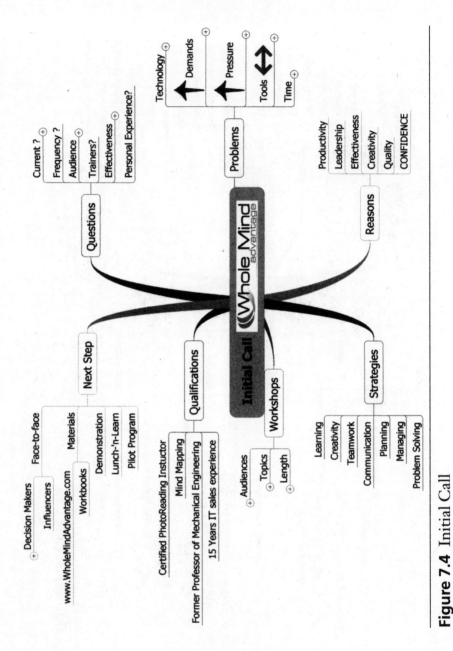

Figure 7.4 Initial Call

The original Initial Call map is too large for this book. I minimized some of the branches on this map for the sake of space. For the full color version of Andrei's map go to www .IdeaMappingSuccess.com.

IT Project

Next comes the actual meeting with the prospect. This idea map is an example of a solution plan for a technology customer for one of their new applications. Refer to Figure 7.5.

Very often in a complex sales process the customer will expect the sales team to present their recommendations based upon the listening, data gathering, and analysis that is performed in the sales process. So I listened. Based on what I heard, I drew this map on a whiteboard in front of the customers' team (along with some other supporting diagrams not included here).

The development of this idea map happened in that moment with the customer's involvment, and it became a graphic representation of the solution presentation meeting. The map shown in Figure 7.5 was drawn after the meeting using Mindjet software for documentation purposes. Instead of a series of linear slides with bullet points, an idea map can be developed to represent the solution. Of course, the prospect also wanted a copy!

I won the business on the IT project and and was able to establish a stronger relationship with the client for future business.

The original IT Project map is too large for this book. I minimized some of the branches in Figure 7.5 for the sake of

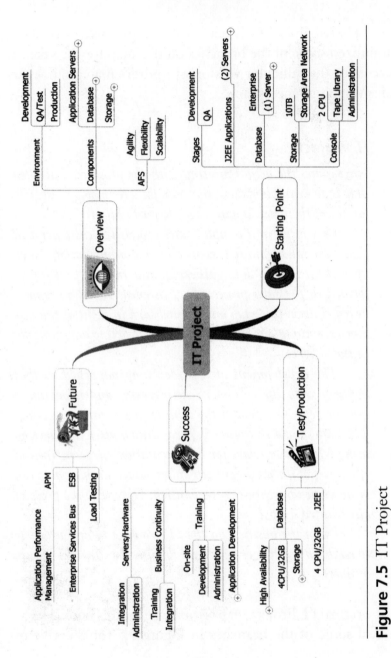

Figure 7.5 IT Project

space. For the full color version of Andrei's IT Project go to www.IdeaMappingSuccess.com.

Simulator Project

M. Kumar is a Project General Manager for the BP Cherry Point Refinery in Blaine, Washington. His backgound is in chemical engineering and business. Following is a desciption of his idea map.

> *This project is our plan to build a simulator for each operating unit in the refinery. This will help the operators to practice many procedures on a simulator rather than on a live unit. It will prepare them to run the unit in a safe manner and respond to emergencies in a competent fashion. Project teams use this map to keep track of various stages of the project (Appraise, Select, Define, Execute, and Operate) and to ensure that the critical milestones, deliverables, and risks are addressed. We use the idea map to communicate the status of the project and the full project picture to the refinery. We utilize a color scheme to reflect progress, concerns, and other issues. The software enables us to take one map and shrink or expand it for the needs of a specific audience during various presentations on this project.*

The original Simulator Project map is too large for this book. I minimized the detail branches in Figure 7.6 to give you an overview of his map. Go to www.IdeaMappingSuccess.com to see Kumar's entire map in color.

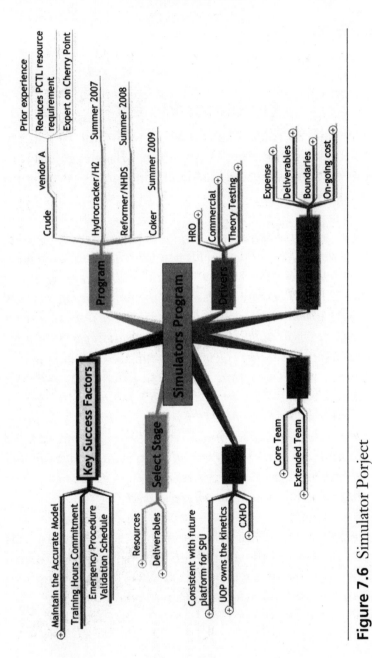

Figure 7.6 Simulator Porject

Fiscal Year 2005 Summary

I introduced Pete Wilkins in Chapter 6 with his giant book maps. This time he created an idea map using Mindjet software to provide his leadership team at Deloitte with an overview of his accomplishments for the fiscal year 2005. Refer to Figure 7.7. Pete shared that this map provided the following benefits:

- *It was easy to see the clients I worked with throughout the year.*
- *The activities and services I provided for each client are clear and grouped by account.*
- *Clear separation of nonclient duties.*
- *Easy to understand revenue numbers by client.*
- *The document can easily be exported to PowerPoint if need be.*

Pete's original map is too large for this book (everything he does is BIG!). I minimized the detail branches in Figure 7.7 to give you an overview of his map. This software feature was a benefit because it enabled me to show you at least part of the map in this book. Go to www.IdeaMappingSuccess.com to see his entire map in color.

Chief Knowledge Officer (CKO)

Trygve Duryea is the chief knowledge officer for The Leadership Group in Santa Barbara, Califonia. He is a huge fan of idea mapping and uses it to run his businesses. He is going to

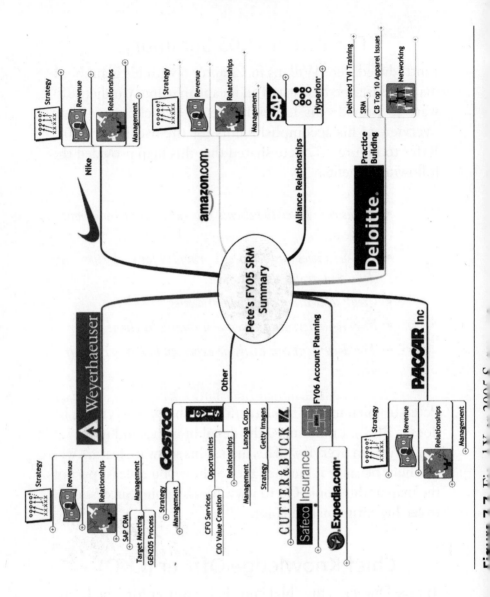

Figure 7.7 ...

share an application he calls the CKO (Chief Knowledge Officer™). Refer to Figure 7.8 as he tells his story.

A manager or business owner known as the chief knowledge officer is the individual that has all the current pertinent information of their company or department at their fingertips. It doesn't mean that reports are only available daily, weekly, quarterly, or monthly. It means every bit of information required to make any decision is available at anytime and anywhere. It means that you will never be without the data to make a decision, to have a knowledgeable conversation, to process an issue, or to capitalize on an opportunity to share information about your company—ever!

The CKO as a management tool is an idea map that is highly effective in communicating the information and knowledge one needs to know anytime, anywhere, within two strokes of the keyboard or mouse. Its main branches and sub-branches are populated with the reports, documents, databases, papers, presentations, and other important information you (and your team members) feel are needed to run the company. Two important elements of the CKO are (a) it delivers to you the information you think is important to make decisions and run the company, and (b) keeping the information correct, current, and up to date is the responsibility of your direct reports and team members—NOT yours. I have the people who are responsible for the varying parts of the business (which links to my map) make their updates every Thursday by 3:00 PM. That keeps me from chasing down new information.

The CKO is available electronically through the map as well as printed and put into a three-ring binder. These CKOs

143

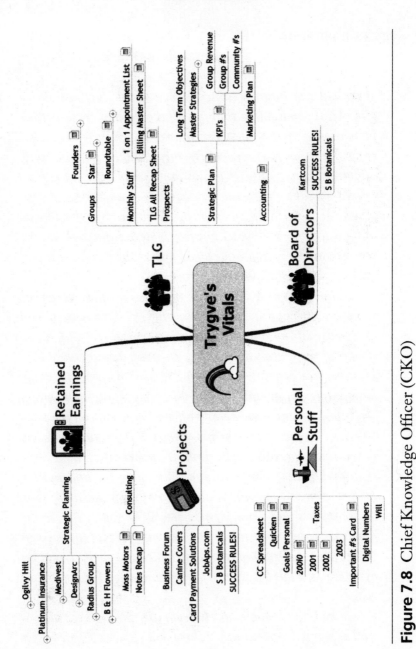

Figure 7.8 Chief Knowledge Officer (CKO)

give the CEOs every bit of information they need to run their company at their fingertips. I can be in any meeting and answer any questiont[sic] about just [about] anything within a second through the CKO map or—if I don't have my laptop with me—the three-ring binder. I use it many times a day and everyone is impressed when I pull up the information at a moment's notice (faster than the managers who should know the information better than I do). I use it to run my CEO think-tank business and consulting practice, and I have developed about 15 other CKOs to help other CEOs run their companies.

Having all the knowledge and information about your company or department at your fingertips doesn't equate to being a micro-manager. It's a signature of leadership that motivates a team to the measured goals and objectives that keeps the company or department focused and on track.

The CKO is the WOW factor of leadership. WOW, where did you get that information? WOW, how did you know that so fast? WOW, you're so organized! WOW, you know a lot about everything! WOW, I didn't know you knew that. WOW, you sure know everything that goes on around here! WOW, you have all the right information to make the right decision and so fast. WOW, I want to know what you know! WOW, I better be on my toes because you know more about my department than I do. WOW!

When creating a CKO, the most important aspect of developing the map is defining the critical information to put in it, identifying where that information comes from, knowing who will be held accountable for updating the information, determining how often the information will be updated, and deciding who will have access to your CKO.

Here are some questions and processes to work through before you start creating your personal CKO idea map.

1. *Set your objective for having a CKO.*
2. *Answer the question, "How will I use this tool?"*
3. *List all the reports you review or have on your desk (daily, weekly, monthly, quarterly, and annually).*
4. *List the departments that have key information.*
5. *Identify the specific information you want from those departments.*
6. *List documents or databases that you refer to periodically.*
7. *List any other information you may want available. This might include personal taxes, outside board of directors, personal investments, memberships, family documents, and activities.*

The chief knowledge officer map keeps me informed at every level of my business without being intrusive, yet at the same time giving me information to make critical and knowledgeable decisions. I think differently with it, and can't imagine running this company without it.

Trygve's original CKO is too large for this book. I minimized the detail branches in Figure 7.8 to give you an overview of his map. Go to www.IdeaMappingSuccess.com to see his entire map in color.

Suggested Activities

Now you have seen multiple applications using Mindjet Pro 6 software. See Figure 7.9 for a summary of the chapter. Your assignment is to download a trial version of Mindjet software (www.mindjet.com) and create at least one electronic map before reading Chapter 8. Here are a few suggestions:

1. You may want to try transferring a completed hand-drawn map into the software. This will give you some practice without having to think about the content of the idea map.

2. Add some images and icons to your map from the library of symbols.

3. Make at least one hyperlink to one of your existing documents or a website.

4. Create some text notes for a branch.

5. Have fun!

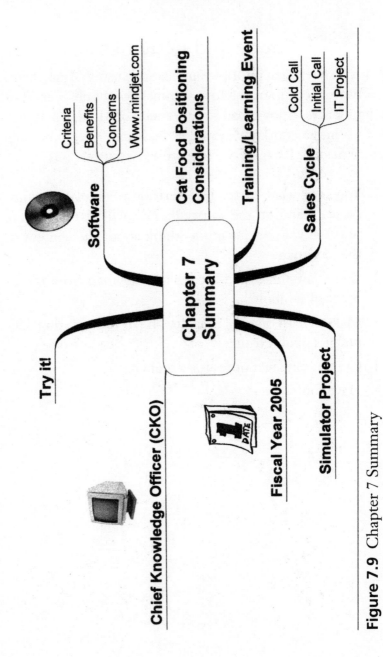

Figure 7.9 Chapter 7 Summary

It's a Process

Now you have seen multiple examples of hand-drawn or software-generated idea maps. Sometimes it can be intimidating to see others' maps (especially those that have beautiful imagery). When first learning how to create idea maps, I remember feeling that I had such a long way to go before I would be able to master the skill. It's possible that your own mapping skills still feel a bit unnatural. Don't worry—that's normal at this point. This chapter will cover the following topics:

- Learning any new skill takes good lessons, time, persistence, and the right model.

- Three individuals will share their idea-mapping journeys. You will see their progression of maps and hear their words of wisdom.

- Finally, I'll cover some typical questions and comments I receive regarding idea mapping.

Learning a New Skill

I wish I had kept copies of my first few maps. They were dreadful. I'm disappointed I can't entertain you with them! Yet with practice, I improved. It is amazing to see how individuals' skills and styles take shape over time. It also gives a sense of accomplishment to look back and see the progress. I've heard skeptics say, "This idea mapping takes too long to learn." I disagree. Mapping is an easy skill that can be taught quickly. The challenge is persisting long and frequently enough that the tool becomes as natural for you as linear note taking. That's what takes some time and patience.

I learned to golf from a friend of mine after we signed up for a company scramble. She was a novice herself, but took me to the driving range for her version of a crash course in golfing. As a result, I learned some bad habits. For the next 5 years I faithfully practiced and reinforced those habits and wondered why my score did not improve. Then I married an avid golfer. The summer after the wedding Kevin signed us up for professional lessons—mostly for my benefit. The instructor changed my stance, my grip, and my swing—and that was just the beginning. I was overwhelmed, I felt awkward, and when I went out to play nine holes my scores were worse than prior to my lessons! It's at this point that I've seen many people quit golf (or the learning of any new skill), and I was tempted right then to do the same. Fortunately, I did not quit, but my scores didn't improve until the new techniques became natural and comfortable instead of new and awkward. They eventually did get better (a little) as I put the time into practicing.

You may experience something similar in the process of learning to create idea maps. Give yourself a break! How long have you been taking linear notes? Are you that surprised that idea mapping feels strange? Remain patient and persistent. The results will be worth it. I recommend keeping your first maps and several others along the way. This will encourage you by providing a documented history of improvement and growth. My friend who taught me to golf did not provide me with a good model. You on the other hand, have already seen excellent idea-mapping models throughout Chapters 6 and 7 (with more to come!). The only part of the success formula that is missing for you right now is time and persistence.

Lesson Ten—
Be patient with yourself.
You're learning a new skill!

What follows is a series of idea-mapping examples from two individuals. I think it is important for novice mappers to see how this skill evolves with perseverance. What seems awkward today will seem easy tomorrow. These maps should be an encouragement to you. The individuals sharing their maps are willing to show you some of their first attempts in order to help you with your learning.

The Journey for Beth Schultz

Dr. Beth Schultz O.D., M.S. Clinical Pharmacology, is an assistant professor teaching at the Pennsylvania College of Optometry (PCO)—the leading school of optometry in the United States. We met when I taught an idea-mapping workshop to nearly all the faculty at PCO. (See Figures 8.1 through 8.5 for the progression of Beth's maps.) Notice the transformation from her first map (where she writes upside down, has no images, and uses no color) to the last map (where hierarchies are clearer; color and imagery is present; and she's implemented a creative connection and coding scheme to enhance recall). She briefly describes each map and then shares some words of wisdom about her learning.

Chemical Warfare (Figure 8.1)

At this point, I had heard only a description of the concept of idea mapping from an international student. I had not yet read any books on the guidelines of mapping, but thought it would be a useful tool for studying. As a student in a part-time master's degree program for pharmacology, I took a challenging course called "Toxicology." The toxicology lecture topic centered in the idea map is Chemical Warfare Agents. The professor presented the material chronologically according to history of use. My numbering of these major events represents the chronological order. For instance:

1. *Criteria for Chemical Warfare Agent Development.*
2. *Mustard Gases.*
3. *Agents Developed by Lee Lewis (never used—war over).*
4. *Nerve Gases.*
5. *Phosgene.*

I must have learned the information since I got an A+ on the exam! Here are a few key points that I learned about idea mapping from this example:

- *The critical need to use CAPITAL letters for major branches to distinguish them from minor branches.*

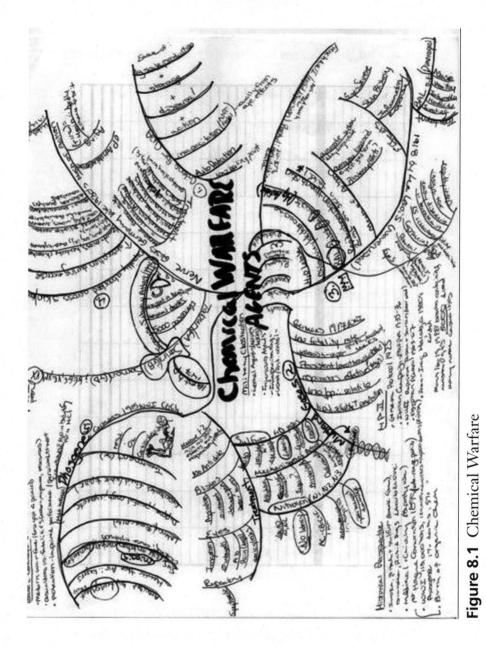

Figure 8.1 Chemical Warfare

- *The value of using single words or shorter phrases for each branch to condense information from sentences into key ideas.*

Antihistamines (Figure 8.2)

As I completed my master's program in clinical pharmacology, I began to teach the pharmacology course at the PCO. One of the first lectures I gave to the students was on the topic of Antihistamines. I made this map in order to create the lecture handout and presentation. The idea map covers the use of antihistamines to treat allergies.

Histamine is released from mast cells so I drew a picture of a mast cell to look like a flag coming off the mast of a boat. Off the mast cell "flag" are three major branches according to the type of antihistamine. Available types are H1, H2, and H3 according to the type of histamine receptor to which it binds. H1 binds to blood vessels—hence the red circle; H2 binds to parietal cells of the stomach—hence the digestive tract; and H3 binds to nerves in the central nervous system— hence the brain and spinal cord. A fourth major branch represents mast cell stabilizers, which are also used to treat allergies by preventing histamine release from the mast cell.

Here are a few key points that I learned about idea mapping from this example:

- *The importance of color to distinguish different types of items.*
- *The enormous benefit of drawing pictures to trigger detailed memories of the concepts.*

155

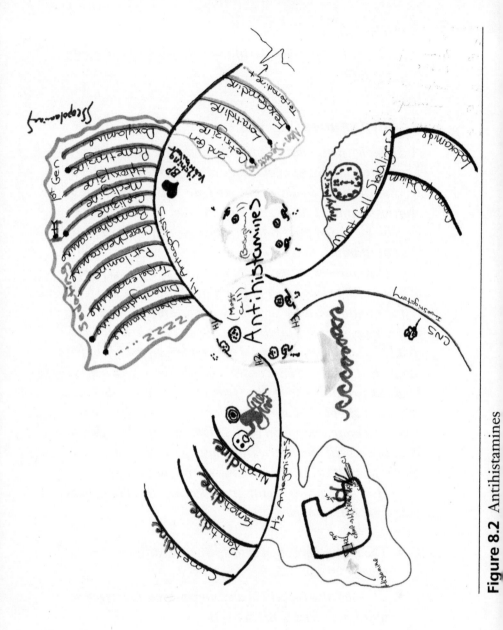

Figure 8.2 Antihistamines

Antianemia Drugs (Figure 8.3)

This map immediately followed the Antihistamine map. I enjoyed mapping my lectures as opposed to generating traditional outlines because it allowed for boundless creativity with color, pictures, [and] connections with other courses and course instructors through shared fundamental concepts. Traditional outlines seemed to truncate my ideas, limit how I could present them in class, and isolate my topic from other instructors' materials that were closely intertwined with mine. It seemed natural to create my word document handout and PowerPoint presentation from my maps.

This idea map views the treatment of anemia according to the type of anemia or blood dyscrasia. For instance, the major branches include: Iron deficiency, Folic Acid deficiency, Vitamin B12 deficiency, Erythropoietin deficiency, and Sickle Cell anemia. For each type of anemia there is one type of treatment aimed at replacing or supplementing the deficient entity.

Here are a few key points that I learned about idea mapping from this example:

- *The value of representing central ideas with a picture to emphasize that everything else radiates from this topic.*

- *I created an inventive use of a specialized color-coding system to represent common domains. To describe characteristics of drugs we apply them back to the domains of Pharmacology: Pharmacodynamics, Pharmacokinetics, Therapeutic Uses, and Adverse Effects, so I assign a color to each domain to increase recall.*

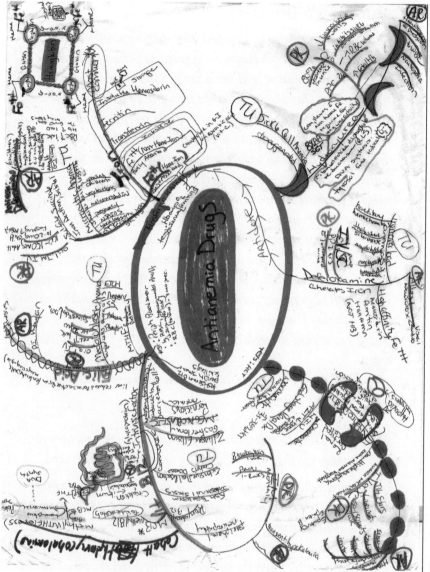

Figure 8.3 Antianemia Drugs

Antihypertensives (Figure 8.4)

I made the Antihypertensive map for my next lecture. The central idea here is that the changes to the peripheral blood vessel can cause hypertension or raise blood pressure. So I drew a blood vessel with this problem. Inside the blood vessel, I drew a staircase to show the different stages of hypertension according to levels of blood pressure measurement. From that abnormal problem, all the major branches off the blood vessel correspond to different types of drug classes used to treat hypertension by regulating the blood vessel.

Here are a few key points that I learned about idea mapping from this example:

- *The value of print size to establish uniformity amongst major branches (larger print) and subbranches (smaller print).*

- *The use of overlapping color to recognize names with the same suffix. Since drugs from the same class often have the same suffix, this shared color overlap helps in recalling them as members of the same class.*

Antianginals (Figure 8.5)

A month after the Antihypertensives lecture I was assigned to give another lecture on Antianginals. I had done some more reading on mapping to gather methods to improve memory retention for both my students and me.

For the Antianginals map I drew an upper body as the central image. Inside the chest is a painful heart resulting from a lack of oxygen caused by arteriosclerosis and/or coronary

159

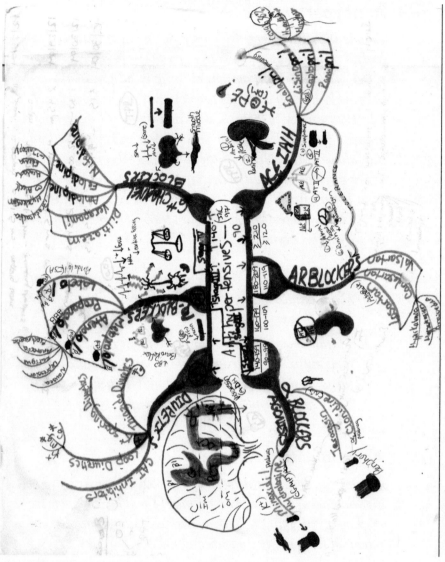

Figure 8.4 Antihypertensives

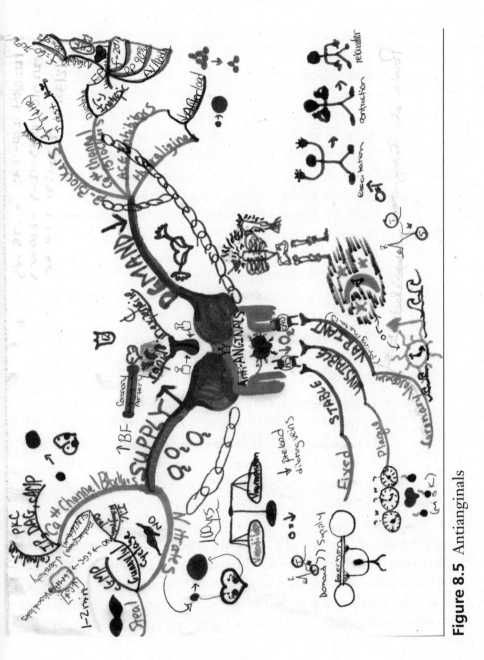

Figure 8.5 Antianginals

artery disease. Below the causes are the types of angina. Above the heart coming off the shoulders are the two strategies used to treat the lack of oxygen to the heart: increase the supply of oxygen and/or reduce the demand on the heart. Branching off that are the drugs that are used based on those respective strategies. Above the neck is a tongue with a bottle to show that these drugs are usually placed under the tongue for quick relief of chest pain. Also, chains are drawn linking several drugs that are used in combination with each other.

Here are a few key points that I learned about idea mapping from this example:

- *The comfort gained (to your neck) by writing all branches on a horizontal plane rather than spinning the page upside down!*

- *How to connect ideas that may be on opposite sides of your map by drawing a simple connecting object—like a chain link.*

- *Using multiple colors for the central idea can accentuate its role. I discovered a higher percentage of recall after seeing a picture versus a word, so I drew pictures to describe all the mechanisms of the diseases, the mechanisms of the drugs, how the drugs are administered, and the mechanisms of the adverse effects of the drugs.*

I recently returned to PCO. This time I was teaching the idea-mapping workshop to their first-year optometry students. They are required to absorb overwhelming amounts of information, and we knew that idea mapping would help them in this task. Beth joined me as a guest speaker and shared this series of maps with the students. As a result, the students are creating idea maps, asking Beth lots of questions, and requesting that Beth and other faculty members share their maps as part of their lectures.

The Journey for Debbie Showler

Debbie Showler is an Advanced Business Analyst working for a large information technology company outside of Toronto, Ontario. I initially met Debbie in 1991 when I was teaching a leadership course in Canada. Debbie and I met again in June of 1992 when she attended one of my *Mind Matters* workshops. The major topics in that course were learning, creativity, and idea mapping. It happened to be one of the first *Mind Matters* workshops I ever taught. Her learning and idea maps were outstanding in so many ways that it prompted me to stay in touch with her. Debbie's journey has been one I have followed for over 14 years.

It was difficult to decide what part of this book would provide the vehicle for her to impact you, the reader, in the greatest way. She is one of the best "real-time" mappers I've ever met (you will learn more about that skill in Chapter 13). Her artistic skills have grown in amazing ways. She has mastered the art of creating and teaching idea mapping, and I treasure the words of wisdom she will share with you. Meet my friend Debbie. (Refer to Figures 8.6 through 8.10 as she describes her maps.)

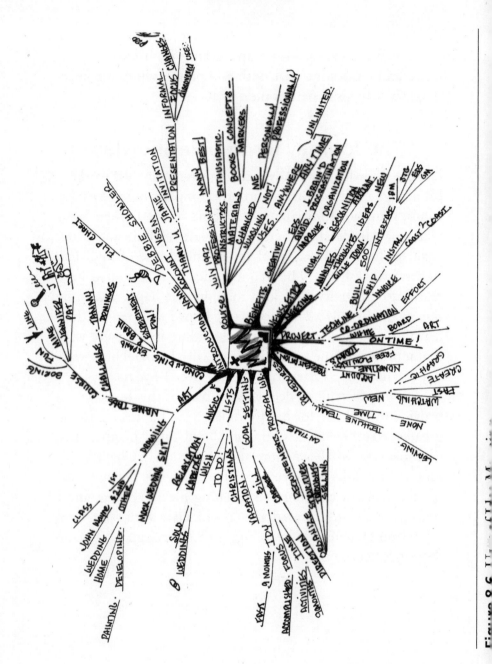

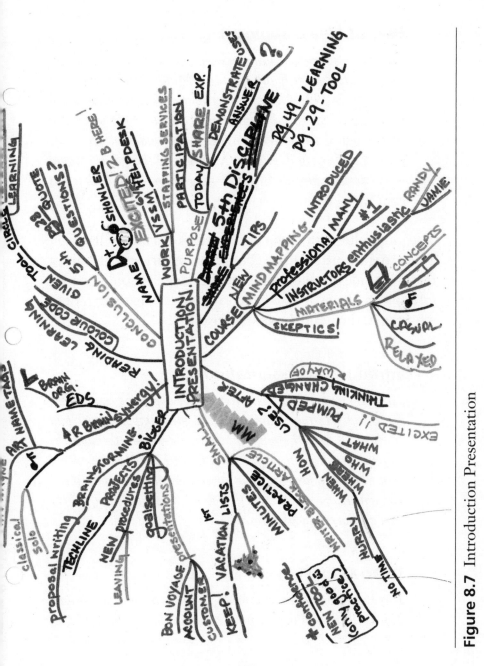

Figure 8.7 Introduction Presentation

Uses of Idea Mapping (Figure 8.6)

A fabulous journey! I look back on this early map and it returns me to a participant's seat in a Mind Matters workshop I attended in 1992. Not long after that, I created this map and used it as an overhead transparency to share my uses of idea mapping with students in a subsequent Mind Matters workshop. Angular, rigid, and constraining are the words I would use to describe this early map compared to the style that has evolved.

The only color in this map besides black is a hint of light red added to the central image. The lines are very straight, and a few are upside down in this example. There are only a handful of images compared to her current style of mapping. Let's move on to the next map in her series.

Introduction Presentation (Figure 8.7)

This map was for a presentation I gave about the results that the Mind Matters course and the idea-mapping tool had given me. I used the map to walk the audience through the content. The lines are still straight, but I added more color. I didn't keep a consistent color for each branch. At the time, I was not aware of the benefit behind that guideline. There were still very few pictures.

To Do Map (Figure 8.8)

This is an idea map of everything I had to do for a single day. This is likely well over a hundred maps later, and you'll see

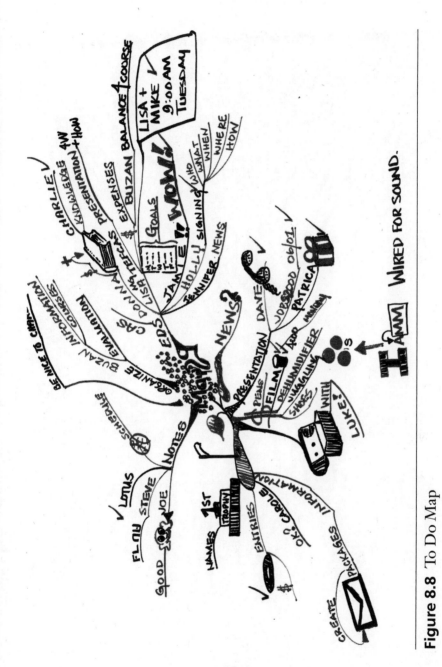

Figure 8.8 To Do Map

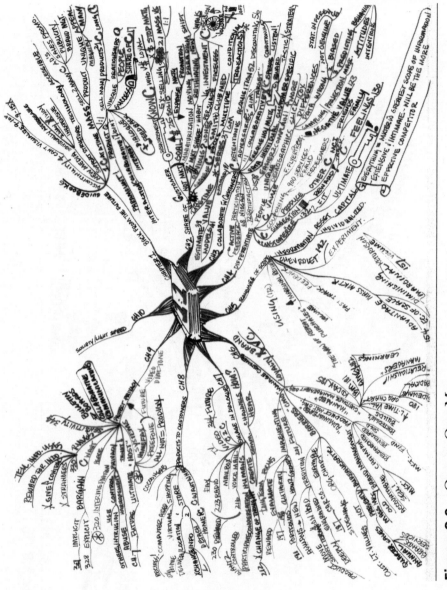

Figure 8.9 One to One Map

how the style is more fun and organic. The central image is a lilac because they bloom here in May. You'll see more appropriate use of color and increased use of images. I'm feeling a real confidence now!

One to One Map (Figure 8.9)

The need to learn and assimilate large amounts of information is what drove the creation of many maps of books and text documents. Using this tool in conjunction with speed-reading is a powerful combination that produced many valuable maps for me. I use them as a reference tool and for learning volumes of information. This example is an idea map of a book titled The One to One Future *by Don Pepper and Martha Rogers. It displays 10 chapters and over 344 pages of information on one page. I color-coded page numbers I thought I might need to refer to at some point in the future*

Corporate Vision (Figure 8.10)

Have you seen a vision statement as an idea map before? This represented the core values, behaviors, and business of this organization. This map was used as the primary communication tool to share and support that vision. A copy of this map was then distributed to the team members of this organization.

From 1992 until now, this has been a tool that I frequently draw upon in my personal and professional life. I have created thousands and thousands of idea maps to this point and cannot recall any two that have turned out exactly the same. It's been a tool to develop a strong business plan, purchase a

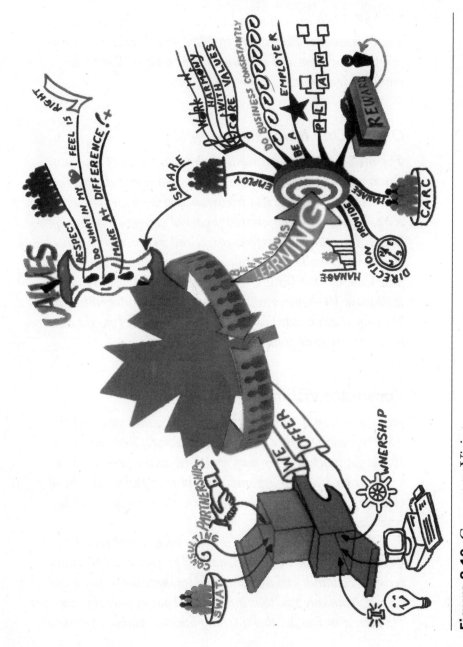

Figure 8.10 Corporate Vision

home, plan my day, organize my thoughts, and to solve many of life's small and big challenges.

The creation of each map is a fun learning process. I have learned to listen and look for key words or phrases that capture the essence and root of the subject at hand. Eventually I became an instructor of idea mapping and a master trainer of this technique for my employer. This gave me opportunities to share the benefits of and to further the use of this amazing thinking tool! Today my maps are a more creative, fluent, and fun reflection of ideas. I feel it's a more playful display of my brain and its limitless capabilities. I can hardly wait to see what the next 1,000 maps give me!

Notice the difference from Debbie's first idea map to the last one shown in Figure 8.10. She went from black and white to color, from no images to virtually all images, and from a linear look to an organic look. Over the years, her maps and their applications have captured vast amounts of complex information. For the new mapper, these maps can be a bit intimidating. Remember, Debbie (and some of the others who share their maps in this book) has been using this tool for 14 years. Be patient. It's a process.

Carey Grow

My very first client was American Bankers Association (ABA) out of Washington, D.C. I met Carey in the first of several workshops I taught for that organization. She was an associate director for ABA and a self-proclaimed skeptic. During the class, I recommended that participants track their idea-mapping progress through their first 100 maps.

Carey actually did just that. What follows is a description of Carey's journey through her 100 maps. She sent me this note only 2 months after the end the course.

Since the class in May of 1996, my life has changed dramatically. I came to the workshop for just another "fluff" class and was prepared with an exit excuse should it turn out to be a nonproductive session. The result? Previously held intellectual paradigms were shattered and inaccurate preconceptions were dispelled. I am writing to share this amazing transformation.

Idea mapping has turned out to be a golden key with which I have unlocked so many exciting opportunities for myself. This is somewhat ironic considering I demonstrated such reluctance to experience this new thought process. Since the class, I have completed 65 out of the 100 recommended maps. It does get easier with practice. It has become so second nature to me now that I am literally mapping every major decision and task in my life.

As mentioned before, idea mapping was a difficult concept for me to embrace. The habit of linear outlining was definitely deeply ingrained. At first, it felt silly and childlike; but a little voice in my head wouldn't let me condemn this concept without giving it an honest try.

First, I bought a set of 36 colored markers to replace my black pen and number 2 pencil. Somewhere around map number 16, the process switched from being silly to being fun. I found freedom with map number 27. Map number 27 represented the tangible, feasible pursuit of unrealized dreams that I had banished to the bottom of my mental hope chest.

Since map number 27, the process has switched from being childlike to being inspiring. Map number 27 helped me realize that most of my "limitations" and phobias regarding my own capabilities had been self-imposed or superimposed by a variety of societal systems.

Most importantly, I have started to grow again as an individual. Instead of viewing myself as half-way done, I now see myself as only half begun. Map number 27 allowed me to envision seven possible new employment avenues. In map number 28, I developed. a proposal for a seminar that sold out within a week and a half after the brochure hit the street. Map number 32 formulated the concept of a professional consortium whereby like-minded individuals could consult with, mentor, and develop each other's strengths.

Map number 38 embodied the manifestation of a secretly held dream which fear prevented me from acknowledging. From the age of 7, I have wanted to be a writer. However, fear of rejection, fear of financial instability, and fear of lack of talent convinced me at an early age that writing was nothing more than a pipe dream. It seems as if everything that I have ever done in my life has been in preparation for this dream; I was just waiting for permission to follow the dream. I now have a book outlined. I have consulted with a literary agent as well as a best-selling writer regarding my potential, and have begun research with local sources to begin formulating the manuscript.

Idea mapping has shown me that anything is feasible. If the mind can think it, it can be mapped—and if it can be mapped, it can be created. Finally, if it can be created, it is therefore possible.

When Carey wrote this note she had made it to map number 65. There was silence for a few months and then she called me when she completed map number 100. I don't remember if it was a particularly profound map or not. I just know that she felt like she had achieved a huge accomplishment and given herself a great gift. The idea-mapping process of learning for Carey was less about how the maps changed over time and more about how this tool led her to new ways of thinking. To this day, I have never seen anyone buy more stickers to put in their maps! Some people will go to all lengths to add images to their maps!

Go to www.IdeaMappingSuccess.com to see color versions of the examples in this chapter.

Questions and Comments

Over the years, I have received a number of recurring questions and comments. You may be wondering the same things, so in the following space are those questions or comments and my responses.

Question #1: Do you find that there are particular types of people who are more open to learning this technique?

Answer: This is probably my number 1 question. People have a tendency to think that this might be best suited for those with learning differences, academic problems, different cultures, younger people, creative individuals, or any other category you can think of. After 15 years of teaching and nearly 15,000 workshop participants, I can only identify one group of individuals who are more open to idea mapping—those who are willing to learn something new. I know it sounds simple, but it's true. It is the only differentiating factor.

Question #2: Do people think you are strange when they see you in a meeting taking notes with colored markers?

Answer: It definitely attracts their interest! However, the maps intrigue most people. The colors, images, and the one-page summary (because they have pages of notes!) attract their attention. I remember attending a meeting about 10 years ago. We took a break, and when I returned to the room, there were four or five people standing around my map deciphering the content of everything covered to that point.

Question #3: How long does it take to become comfortable with idea mapping?

Answer: That depends. Frequency of use and variety of applications enhances comfort. You can't create a map once a month and expect miracles. That is not often enough. I recommend doing several maps each week until it feels more natural.

Question #4: Does your husband use idea maps?

Answer: Yes, he can and does when appropriate. As a registered representative in the securities industry, all presentations must be NASD approved in addition to being approved by his compliance department. However, idea mapping has been a nice supplement to helping him organize and emphasize key points when making formal proposals.

Question #5: Why haven't I heard about this before, and why isn't this taught in schools?

Answer: Some schools and teachers are using various

mapping strategies. More often teachers use a simpler tool called "webbing" or "clustering." Unfortunately, those tools do not take advantage of color or imagery and are rarely applied to subjects beyond language arts. I think the main reason it's not taught and you haven't heard about it is simply because the tool is not well known.

Question #6: When taking notes on written materials, do you read everything first, or map as you read?

Answer: I take a layered approach to written materials. I start by doing what Vanda North calls a "power browse" of the material. Whether it's a book or an article, I quickly view every page—marking the text or figures that catch my eye. This gives me a feel for the content, layout, and complexity of the material. It helps me decide what portions I need to read or if I need to read the material at all! Then I create the main branches. From that point on, I usually map as I read.

Question #7: Are there any statistics on timesavings, productivity gains, or how this technique has helped in schools?

Answer: There are thousands of individual examples of timesavings, productivity gains, and educational benefits. I survey the organizations where I teach anywhere from 30 to 60 days after the workshop. This is how I gather statistics for a particular group. I compile the results and feed that document back to the sponsor of the event. The key is getting enough respondents to make the data statistically relevant. I have created measurement documents for many clients. Below is the cumulative response to one of the survey questions asked to 20 participants who attended my 2-day workshop. This information was gathered 60 days after the course. This is a typical response.

The learning in this class has helped me improve my: (give each skill a rating from 1–5. 1 = Strongly Disagree, 2 = Disagree, 3 = Neutral, 4 = Agree, 5 = Strongly Agree)

 _4.4_ *Ability to be more creative*

 _4.1_ *Ability to learn new skills*

 _4.7_ *Note taking skills*

 _4.1_ *Project management skills*

 _4.1_ *Ability to have more fun on the job*

 _3.9_ *Self-confidence*

 _4.4_ *Brainstorming*

 _3.5_ *Ability to manage change*

 _4.9_ *Idea-mapping skills*

 _4.7_ *Thought organization*

 _4.5_ *Planning skills*

 _4.0_ *Job performance*

 _4.25_ *Productivity*

 _4.2_ *Memory*

 _4.1_ *Motivation*

 _4.25_ *Break problems into smaller components*

One of the most astounding statistics I've personally witnessed was when I was teaching a group of 55 students and 10 teachers from Willow Run High School in Ypsilanti, Michigan. I met with this group three times over a period of

3 months. Sharon Maynard, who at that time was one of the school counselors, measured student grade point averages (GPAs) before the sessions and then at the end of the semester. The average GPA increased nearly half a point.

Question #8: How can I teach my children to idea map and how old should they be?

Answer: If children can draw, they have all the necessary skills. I wouldn't force it on them. As they watch you create a map (especially if you are using colored markers), it will stir their curiosity. Once you have their interest, have them pick a topic. It could be themselves, a hobby, the family, their pet, or what they did that day. Just like adults, they may get frustrated with their drawing, so encourage their patience. Once they master something simple, then you can introduce using it for some of their schoolwork! Creating book reports, history lessons, foreign language—the list of possibilities is endless.

Question #9: What is the most unusual map you ever created?

Answer: I would have to say that my hurricane Wilma evacuation plan has to be the most unusual map for me. In October 2005 I was certifying a group of 17 idea-mapping instructors from all over the world that could potentially get stranded in Florida, and it was unknown as to whether we would be forced to evacuate. What would be the criteria for evacuation? If we had to evacuate, where would we go and how would we get there? If we stayed, how would we plan for food, water, and communication? There was another group flying in from all over the world (Australia, Singapore, Hong Kong, Italy, Canada, and the United States) for a class the following week. How would we notify those still flying in about our evacuation location? Should we cancel that class after they had prepared for months? These were some of the questions I struggled through while creating this map along with one of the other participants.

We ended up not evacuating based on the criteria and the fact that we were not asked to by the state police. The certifications continued the following week without electricity or water, since the storm hit much stronger than expected. It was an amazing opportunity for creativity and an incredibly memorable experience for all of us. Someday I'll share our recipe for Hurricane Salad!

Now the activities are going to get more challenging. The next chapter will introduce you to an advanced application of idea mapping called the Team Mapping Process. Figure 8.11 gives a summary of this chapter.

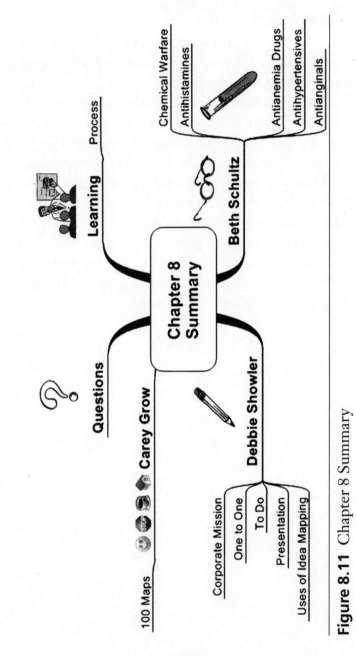

Figure 8.11 Chapter 8 Summary

Team Mapping Method

S ome of the most exhilarating and nerve-racking work I do is to facilitate teams through the process of creating, sharing, consolidating, and prioritizing their ideas around a real issue. It is exhilarating because the people involved in the process get excited. Invariably the outcome is much better than the traditional brainstorming session we have all experienced. It's also nerve-racking because there's little I can do to prepare for these sessions, it's very difficult to judge the timing, and I have no control over the outcome. The only thing I can do is review the process and objective prior to the session, clearly explain the process to the group, make sure everyone understands the topic or issue at hand, and manage the personalities and emotions of the participants. In addition, I try to make it fun.

Much of my work using this method is in the area of strategic planning, although you can use this technique any time a team of people are contributing ideas for a common purpose. As I walk you through the process, imagine that you are participating in this session with your team and I am the facilitator. Here is what this chapter will cover:

- Defining the Topic
- Individual Idea Map
- Suggestions
- First Consolidation
- Second Consolidation

- Prioritization
- Taking Action
- Review and Update
- Benefits
- Your Assignment

Defining the Topic

Having a clear and shared understanding of the topic is absolutely critical to the success of this process. I have participated in many meetings and discussions where the purpose, the issue, or the topic was never clearly defined. The funny thing is that I don't know if the participants ever realized the lack of definition. But the frustration was certainly evident. When this is the case there is confusion, people are attempting to solve the wrong problem, discussions get off track, and time is wasted. The other problem I've seen is when groups try to tackle multiple topics at the same time. I understand that sometimes the complexity of the issue requires doing this, but whenever possible take one topic at a time. The more you can simplify the topic (even if the subject itself is complex) the better. I've also seen attempts to simplify the topic turn into having too vague a topic. This brings us to Lesson 11, which is:

Lesson Eleven—
Clearly identify a single, simple, and specific topic for the
Team Mapping Method.

One last comment about the topic: How many times do you see teams head off on some project that doesn't meet the objectives or vision of the organization? Take the time upfront to share with the team the importance of the issue and how it ties to the vision or purpose of the organization or project. It will provide an even greater context for and commitment to the process that is to be followed.

Individual Idea Map

Once the topic is defined, each person independently creates an idea map of everything they can possibly think of relating to the topic. In the case of an annual strategic planning session, I ask participants to capture thoughts around some of the following categories:

- Current organizational struggles
- Personnel-related issues (i.e., hiring, retention)
- New products and services
- Training
- Customers (current and future)
- Next year's objectives
- Marketing and advertising
- Suppliers
- Finances/budget
- Opportunities
- Cost savings and revenue generation
- Technology
- Processes and work flow
- Recognition
- Production
- Competition

I use this as a way to get individuals thinking, and to encourage their own creative thoughts as well. Even the creation of a central image can help to further clarify the topic when it comes time for the first consolidation. All ideas, words, and concepts are to stay in the map. No editing of ideas should occur at this point.

Lesson Twelve— Always start the team mapping process by asking each participant to create an individual map around the defined topic.

The individual maps are critical to the process. In a typical session when one person throws out an idea, it can draw the whole group into a single train of thought. This is similar to the flow of thoughts introduced in Chapter 2. What needs to occur at this stage is a bloom of ideas (BrainBloom™) that will eventually be used to generate multitudes of possibilities. When this stage is overlooked, participants have a tendency to let the boss or the most influential person guide most of the process. The individual map provides opportunities for some of the more quiet thinkers to add their brilliance into the session.

This part of the process could take some time depending on the size and complexity of the issue the group is tackling. If you foresee this being a lengthy first step, one suggestion might be to have this portion of the task completed as mandatory prework to the session. (If one person doesn't do this, it will affect the rest of the process.) The benefit here is that each person can dedicate whatever time they need. Because of the varying roles of the participants, some will need to spend much longer creating their maps than others. You avoid people waiting around for others to finish. When team members come to the session, have each person take 5–10 minutes to review their maps and make any additions (no deletions) that come to mind.

Whether participants create a quick individual map during the session or they come to the session with their maps, we are now ready for the first consolidation. Before addressing the next step, let me share some suggestions.

Suggestions

Encourage creative thinking. You do not want to put time and energy into a process that achieves average results. Sometimes people get nervous sharing ideas that are far from the norm. This isn't the case when a crisis requires an ingenious solution, so do not let this be the case during the session either. Tell the team to avoid imposing limitations on themselves. Don't let the budget, the boss, the client, or the market deter you from considering any idea. If the idea is that important, maybe the team can discover an inventive solution. An environment of fun can spice things up a bit too. Provide toys, music, colored markers, and healthy snacks. Take breaks every hour or when it seems appropriate based on the flow of ideas and the energy level of the group.

Kill the idea-killer. There is no one more destructive to one of these sessions than the person who shoots down ideas. It only takes one shot and the victim will clam up for the rest of the day. Most idea-killers don't know who they are so it is your responsibility to tell them. Buy some fun toys that make noise and give one to each participant. Then set some ground rules. Tell team members that any time they feel like their idea is being killed, they are to use their noise-maker to make the perpetrator aware of the violation. It will add some humor to the process and make the killer aware of his or her crime.

First Consolidation

The next step is going to be a consolidation of ideas. I suggest 3–4 members per group. Your group may be much larger than this, but try to break it down into smaller groups. We will handle the consolidation of the overall groups' ideas later. You can select the groups based on common areas of work or interest, or you may prefer cross-functional groups. Both have unique benefits, so choose for yourself based on the topic and purpose for this activity.

Start by having each team member share his or her individual maps with his or her group. If during this time of sharing it sparks additional thoughts, add them to your map. This is a time to share—not critique. Use those noisemakers if necessary.

The next step gets a little tricky the first time you try this. The result will be one large idea map that contains all of the information from every member's map. Yes, I do mean *all*. Using large flip-chart paper or the Mindjet software, your task will be to determine a main thought that some of you have in common. This could be your first main branch for the group map. You may even want to create an over-

187

riding word to describe the varying words the group members used for this common thought. It is important at this stage not to assume that two identical words mean the same thing to two people. You need to keep the original context and meaning clear. What I mean by "re-engineering" could be completely different than your meaning or context. Take the time to clarify.

Once the group has identified the first main branch (or branches), look for all the ideas in your map that connect to this thought. Add those ideas to the map. You work your way through this process until all ideas from the maps are in one large map. If new ideas result from the conversations, add them into the map as well. Add images wherever you can. When you're done, take a break.

If there are a large number of individuals participating in this session (5 groups of 4 members each, for example), it is now time for each team to share their map with all who are present. It is likely that you will hear some similar themes between team maps as well as original possibilities. Again, if these presentations spark new ideas, add them to your group map. You will be fascinated by the varying ways teams captured their data. Team members see their ideas captured and valued. People who normally might not share have actively participated in the process.

Second Consolidation

If the original group was only 3–4 individuals, skip to prioritization. If there were multiple groups of 3–4 people, the question needs to be asked, "Is there value in consolidating all of this information?" In most cases, the answer will be yes.

Again, either you will need large paper or you will need to use the Mindjet software while projecting the mega-team map on the screen. Either choose the map that seems to best represent the thoughts of the group and add information from the other group maps to it, or repeat the process used in the first consolidation to build the mega-team map. All ideas are included at this stage as well. This can end up being a very large idea map; however, it is interesting that, after a while, there seems to be a natural consolidation of ideas. People may say, "well this and that are covered here," so those ideas can be removed, and the map starts to tighten up.

Prioritization

Now your group, regardless of size, should be working from a single team map. In the strategic planning sessions I run, there is now a plethora of possible actions that could be taken. It is unrealistic to think that all of these tasks could be accomplished in the next year, so we need to prioritize them.

I usually have people prioritize in two ways. The first way is by defining those tasks that are most critical to the success of the overall organization. The objective of the second prioritization is to identify those tasks that will provide a quick success to the group. These actions are typically easy to implement, low cost, and not requiring of months of approvals. Let's start with the critical success actions.

While everyone can view the mega-map, have each person individually define his or her top five priorities. You may use his or her top three or his or her top eight ideas—you decide based on the volume of data you have to work with. The lower numbers tend to work better because you're ultimately looking for the critical tasks to emerge rather than prioritizing every item on the map. Once everyone is ready, the facilitator will start by having the first person share his or her rankings. Using a single color (if using a hand-drawn map), the facilitator should place a "1" by the branch this person states as his or her number one priority, "2" by the branch this person states as his or her number two priority, and so on. Go around the room until all have provided their rankings.

Do another individual prioritization to identify the top three to five quick successes. If using a hand-drawn map, the facilitator will choose a different color to collect the rankings this time. If using the software, simply add a branch called *Quick Success*, followed by a branch with all the rankings. There are many other ways within the software that you can distinguish the critical actions from quick successes. Choose one that seems easiest for you. If it has been an hour or so since the last break, take another one now. This process can be exciting, but mentally draining.

Taking Action

Now you have a visual of the priorities. Notice if any quick successes and critical actions overlap. Observe where most participants agree on the priorities, and identify the top actions in each category. Notice that no ideas were eliminated. They just didn't make it into the top lists—yet. This is a major benefit, as people do not experience the rejection of the idea. These possibilities are still on the map and can be revisited at some point in the future. I'll discuss review periods shortly.

Start with one of the top actions. Have each person create an individual map on the implementation of this idea. The maps could include any of the following thoughts and more:

- Deadlines
- Project team members
- Stakeholders
- Training
- Strengths, weaknesses, opportunities, threats
- Research
- Costs/pricing/budget/revenue
- Customer involvement
- Project scope
- Communication plan
- Impacts
- Project purpose and goals

Once the individual maps are complete, merge these maps by following the steps in the first consolidation. The implementation plan for critical actions and quick successes can be created with the larger group (which may require a second consolidation) or you may decide to leave the development of this plan to a group of individuals that will be affected by or eventually implement the plan.

Review and Update

Before leaving the prioritization session, set a date and time for review of the progress and status of the actions. Keep the team maps and use them in the review process. Update these maps with any progress. Eventually you will finish these tasks and need to set new priorities. Maybe some of the items that didn't get addressed initially will become more of a priority now. On the other hand, if business has changed and much time has passed, you may have to start from scratch with a fresh look at the topic at hand.

Benefits

The benefits of this process are many. Although it is a time commitment to work through these consolidations, there will be shared understanding, teamwork, a boost in morale, and ultimately timesavings. The clarity alone will bring common vision to the task. These team maps can act as communication tools when sharing with other departments or stakeholders. Post them on the wall to show the status of the project.

Finally, the idea maps reduce what I call verbal redundancy. Have you ever attended a meeting where the participants repeatedly share their comments on a topic that has already been addressed? I think some people just like to hear themselves talk. With the map in front of the group, all you need to do is point to that particular area of discussion and ask if anyone has any additional thoughts. Otherwise, you can gently move on to another topic.

Your Assignment

Find an opportunity for making a decision that will involve at least one other person. It may not be as involved or elaborate as the process described in this chapter. Experimenting on a smaller scale using a topic that is not emotionally charged can give you some exposure to the team mapping process. Start small and work your way up to a larger, more complex subject.

Now that you are becoming an expert at the team mapping method, the next chapter is going to show you examples of advanced idea maps that break all the rules! See Figure 9.1 for an idea-map summary of this chapter.

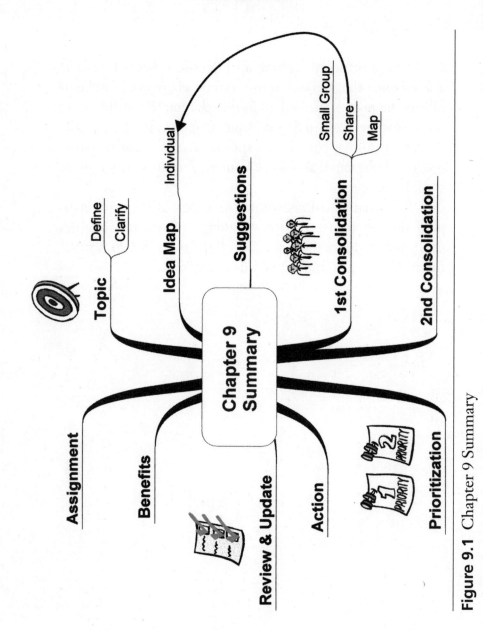

Figure 9.1 Chapter 9 Summary

10

Breaking All
the Rules

In this chapter, you will be encouraged to develop your own style of maps and read about some amazing applications covering the following topics:

- EPA Regulation Summary
- A Book—*Orbiting the Giant Hairball*
- Article Summary in Preparation for a Leadership Development Program (combines software and hand-drawing)
- Real-Time Presentation Note Taking
- The Future
- World Trade Center Memorial Park

Breaking the Rules

The intention of the laws of idea mapping (refer to Chapter 3) is to maximize recall and thought organization, to clearly define associations, to provide opportunities for generating greater quantities of ideas, and to leverage both left and right cortical skills. I recommend following the laws as closely as possible during the early stages of learning, but the intention is not to limit ingenuity. At some point you will have an application where breaking the rules actually provides greater creativity and fulfillment of purpose. Making a conscious choice to do this is part of learning to master some of he more advanced idea-mapping skills. In this chapter, each map example will break some of the rules—or maybe I should say that the creators have taken some artistic liberties. This is intentional. After all, this tool is for you, the author of your map. I encourage you to work and create in a way that will give you pleasure and meet the needs of your application. Have fun with it!

The idea maps in this chapter are also available in color at www.IdeaMappingSuccess.com.

EPA Regulation Summary

This example uses the Mindjet software. The application did not lend itself to the "one word per line" rule. Michael Torpey works on the Diesel Blending Project SPA (Single Point of Accountability), at one of the world's largest energy companies. Refer to Figure 10.1 as he describes this application. Torpey shares,

I am working on a project that will require EPA (Environmental Protection Agency) approval. Two people familiar with the EPA requirements for the project provided me with two contradictory opinions about one of these requirements. I had read the EPA regulation several times, but I was not able to determine who was right, and the format of the published regulation made it difficult to follow. Although it is written in outline form, with numbers and letters separating the various sections, it was written without indentations, which would help to show where one section ends and another begins. I began to summarize the regulation by hand, but decided to use an idea map instead. When the idea map was complete, it proved to be useful for several reasons:

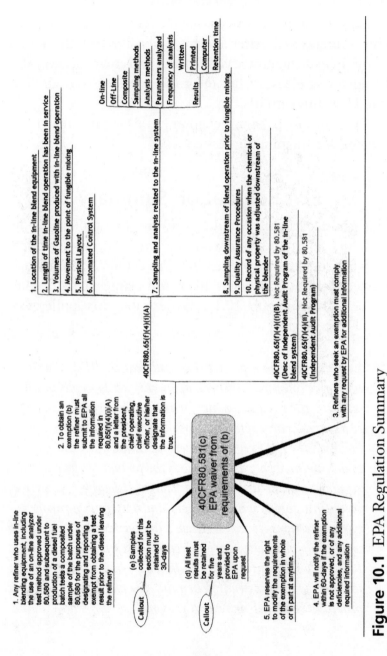

Figure 10.1 EPA Regulation Summary

- *I had the entire section of the EPA regulation summarized on one page.*

- *The pertinent section of the EPA regulation, the requirements for the EPA petition, was summarized in one branch.*

- *I was able to clearly see which requirements were not required for my project.*

A Book—*Orbiting the Giant Hairball*

Megan Clark has held numerous leadership positions within a large automotive company in Michigan. Her expertise is broad and ranges from information technology to organizational development. Her current title is Manager, Program Management Office, Information Technology. She is one of those unique individuals who are both highly technical and highly creative. I met her in 1998 when she brought me into her organization to teach a 2-day workshop. When Megan finds something worthwhile, everyone wants to participate. Because of that class and its success, over 600 employees of this company have attended my workshops to date.

Shortly after attending this class, Megan was at a high-level leadership meeting. During one of the breaks, a prominent member of the management team approached her and said, "Megan, you remind me of a book I just read." Megan was flattered that this man would offer such a compliment. She followed up by asking, "Really? What's the title of the book?" The executive replied, "*Orbiting the Giant Hairball.*"

Her reaction went from thinking she received a great compliment to wondering if she had a corporate future! The conversation was brief and then the meeting reconvened. The only thought in her mind at that point was, "Oh my, what kind of book is that?"

She immediately headed to the bookstore to get a copy of *Orbiting the Giant Hairball* by Gordon MacKenzie. It is a fascinating book written by a former vice president of Hallmark. Thankfully for Megan, the comment from the executive turned out to be quite a compliment.

Megan decided to map the contents of the book as she read. Refer to Figure 10.2 for her map. This is one of those books where boiling down a phrase into a single key word for the map just kills the power of the message. She took some artistic liberties and created an amazing summary of this book. Following are Megan's thoughts about her idea map.

Purpose:

Have you ever read a book that touched you deeply and you wanted to remember every story in it? That was my experience with Gordon MacKenzie's Orbiting the Giant Hairball. *The purpose of creating my idea map was very personal—to help me remember the treasured stories written by Mr. MacKenzie as a way to remind myself that corporate life (yes, even in big, dreary, corporate buildings!) can have meaning and creativity for those of us within the walls!*

Benefits:

- *instant one page recall of all the key messages in the book*
- *easy mechanism to share the author's wisdom with others*

Outcomes:

- *excellent communication mechanism*

- *visual reminder of "corporate grace"*
- *teaching/mentoring tool*

But the story doesn't end there. After completing the map, one of her peers challenged her to send a copy of the map to the author of the book. So she called the phone number in the back of the book to find the address where she could send her map. The voice on the other end of the phone answered, "Gordon MacKenzie." Megan was momentarily speechless because she was not expecting Gordon to answer the phone. Eventually she sent him her map, and he was appreciative of the way Megan was able to capture his message in a visual format.

Megan also refers to this map as a teaching/mentoring tool. During one of the more recent workshops I taught for Megan's organization, there was a participant in the group who was visually impaired. A medical condition made him legally blind at an early age. He had the most incredibly positive attitude. When Megan asked him why he was always smiling, his response was, "Because I remember seeing at a very young age, for me the grass is always green and the sky is always blue." Prior to him leaving the automotive industry, Megan spent several weeks reading *Orbiting the Giant Hairball* to this young man. She cried while reading him the last chapter. Who was impacting whom? I think it was mutual.

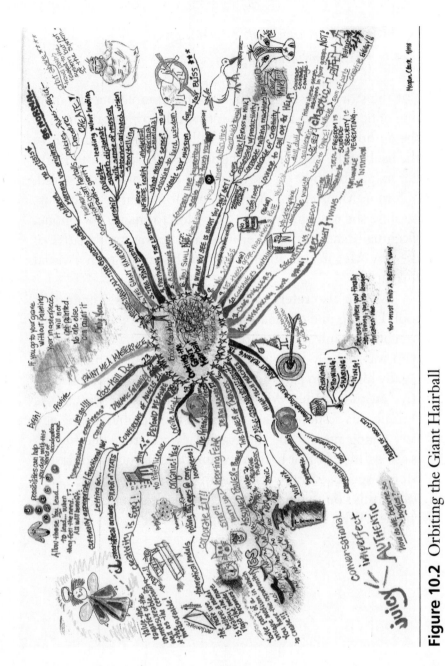

Figure 10.2 Orbiting the Giant Hairball

Article Summary
in Preparation for a
Leadership Development Program

The next map—which can be found in Figure 10.3—combines the use of the software with real-time mapping. Sandy Dietrich is a production superintendent working for a large automotive supplier and has been using idea maps since 1998. Following is the description of her application.

The original map was created using the Mindjet software. It was the summary of an article entitled, "Jack Welch." The article was distributed in preparation for a company-sponsored leadership development program. I took the map of this article to the program. The map already captured most of the presenter's material; therefore, it minimized the note taking during the lecture. Instead of worrying about taking notes during the lecture, I could focus on the presenter's ideas.

The combination of software and real-time note taking saved time. Prior to the lecture, I already had most of the key points in my mind. The presentation reinforced those thoughts instead of introducing them for the first time. This added to my ability to remember important ideas. Instead of pages of notes, the completed map provides an excellent one-page reference with all concepts and the entire theme readily viewable. After the program I displayed it in my office, where it generated interest and conversation.

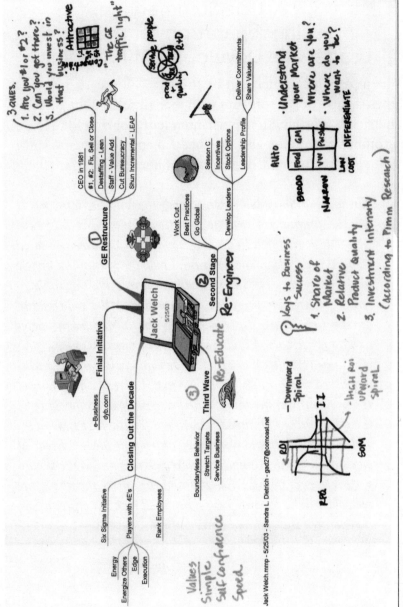

Figure 10.3 Article Summary

Real-Time Presentation Map— Landmark Forum

Choon Boo Lim has served in various senior management positions and is currently a principal lecturer for Ngee Ann Polytechnic in Singapore. He has been mapping since 1996, and he has mastered the advanced skill of capturing data at the moment it is presented. For suggestions on how to create "real-time" maps, see the description in Chapter 12.

Choon Boo attended a Landmark Forum seminar on March 29, 2005, in SPRING.Singapore's Auditorium. (See his idea map in Figure 10.4.) Following is his description of that event and his map:

My good friend, Robert Koh, invited me to this seminar and I decided to accept his invitation. I was not disappointed.

Why did I decide to do an idea map of this session?

In the back of my mind, I was thinking, since I am already at the seminar, it would not cost me anything except listening, drawing some images, and writing down some key words. If the map turns out to be presentable, I would then be able to share it with Robert and anyone interested in this wonderful whole-brain method of taking notes.

Fortunately, the idea map turned out to be really memorable. It provided me with lots of inspirations from the many Landmark Forum graduates, who spoke with tremendous feelings and energy about what they have gained from the course. These comments were captured under the "LESSONS" branches. Of course, needless to say, the speaker, Mr. Jerome, did a wonderful job in explaining the principles involved in the course as well as what many of us have gone

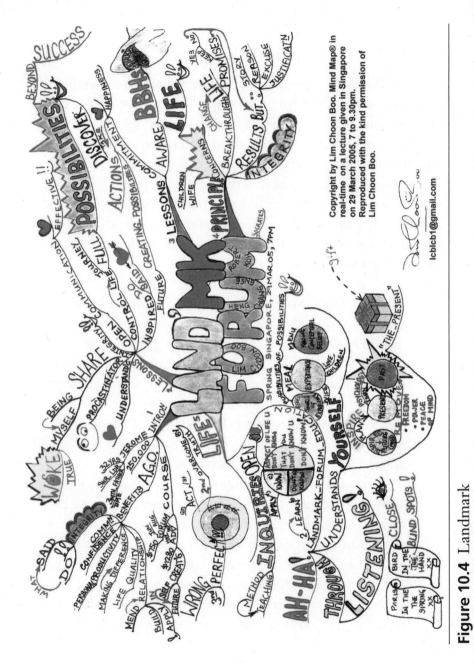

Figure 10.4 Landmark

through in life. I captured that information under the "PRINCIPLES" and "LIFE" branches. I was extremely delighted to have mapped the lecture in real-time.

How did I create the map?

My basic preparation involved bringing along my multi-colored pens, an A4 or A5-sized paper (depending on the type of course or seminar), and arriving early for the presentation so that I could find a good seating location. The latter is important as it helps me see the face of the speaker and clearly hear the emphsis [sic] of the words. I was amazed at how the map unfolded during that seminar.

How many hours of information?

The Landmark Forum map summarised a total of about 2½ hours of presentation (7:00 PM to 9:30 PM). The break provided a great time for the brain to integrate essential information after listening and summarising the key points of the lecture as well as participants' presentations.

How did it benefit me and how did I use it afterwards?

Mapping the lecture benefited me in many ways. I find myself reviewing the lecture from time to time. In particular, the information on the "PAST," "PRESENT," and "FUTURE" branches helps me in finding freedom, power, and peace of mind. This seminar also taught me a lot about "THE PRESENT"—a gift that every one of us should treasure.

A more important benefit arising from my idea map was that I was able to share the knowledge of what I have gained with my many colleagues and friends. On a broader perspective, the idea map helps increase not only an individual's intellectual capital, but also that of an organisation—especially if everyone maps any talk, seminar, or course that they attend.

Last, but not least, the idea map enables me to share my passion and dreams of encouraging everyone [to] learn this wonderful technique.

Choon Boo's map is the original one he created. I don't want anyone to think that he went home and made it beautiful! He has quite a gift for capturing live information. You can view one of his more complicated "real-time" maps at www.Idea MappingSuccess.com. Look for his Robert Kaplan map.

The Future

I met Michael Shaw in October of 2005. He was a participant in my workshop at Mayo Clinic in Rochester, Minnesota. He is currently a second-line manager with responsibility for three computer data centers.

My work at Mayo is unique. The original management team that brought the workshops to Mayo beginning in 2004 requested advanced training and the addition of memory and speed-reading. It requires additional work on the part of those attending to make this possible. As prework for the 2-day workshop, each participant reads a book about idea mapping and then creates a map that I review prior to class. The night before this particular series of classes, I was browsing through the maps when Michael's map caused me to stop and study his work in detail. I felt like he had given me a personal look into his life. His map covers his past as well as his future (see Figures 10.5 and 10.6 for before and after photographs). Because nearly everything in his idea map is an image, it takes some explanation in order for you to understand the map. See Figure 10.7 following his story.

When thinking about the topic to choose for my first idea map, my first instinct was to keep it strictly business. After all, the course would be full of people from our organization of employment. However, because I had gone through two major life changes in the past 3 years, it seemed appropriate to make it personal (The Future inside a crystal ball). This proved to be a good decision as the effect was therapeutic as I drew, and became something I now call my "visual journal."

Seibboh (Hobbies Backwards)

For reasons that will become clearer after describing the "4 Me" branch, hobbies often seem foreign to me—which is why I wrote the root word backwards. This is most likely due to the fact that the majority of my time is spent alone (although I wish it were otherwise). Also it seems foreign because most of my life had been about work. I really didn't allow myself to "waste" time on hobbies.

I was an avid reader all the way from childhood until just a couple years ago (I even read technical manuals and enjoyed them!). Since then reading has been much more difficult in that it doesn't hold my attention. In fact, there have been several times where I can only read a couple sentences on page one and go no further. However, I still do manage to find a couple books a month that I can stick with.

I have a very wide taste in music (CD with musical notes)—classical, blues, rock, reggae, even some country— anything but opera!

I took up fishing this year. Beyond catching bass and trout locally, I took my first trip into Canada this past Labor Day. In addition to catching walleye and northern, I also kayaked (for the first time) around the island our cabins were on.

I own several hundred movies on DVD. Surprisingly, I've never tired of watching the same movie numerous times.

Growing up I had always wanted to go to a professional sports event. I recently attended a Minnesota Wild NHL game (an awesome experience!) as well as a Minnesota Vikings NFL game.

When I came to work for my current employer, I was given opportunities to travel. Often, this coincides with my giving a presentation on my profession—computer data center management. I've traveled to Orlando, Palm Springs, Seattle, Nashville, and Las Vegas. One day I hope to travel to Europe and New Zealand. Although I never followed through on it, this hope stems from the foreign languages I've learned in high school, college, and a previous employer: Spanish, German, French, and Japanese.

The Past

Unarguably, this was the toughest branch for me to draw. I was raised to always achieve something greater than I'd already accomplished, don't settle for second best, and so on. Yet there are some things from my past I have a difficult time accepting.

On the good side, I have an Associate's degree (that's supposed to be a blue graduation cap) from Rochester Community College (RCC) and a Bachelor's degree in Computer

Science from Winona State University (WSU). I completed my Bachelor's while I was working full time for my second employer.

My first job was delivering pizza for Domino's. We ate pizza for dinner every night and to this day, I cannot stand the smell of it. I then left to start work at International Business Machines here in Rochester. I worked there 11 years, starting out in disk-drive manufacturing and ending up a programmer, coding tools to help build the AS/400 operating system.

I left IBM and came to work at the Mayo Clinic, also in Rochester. I've been here for 9 years, starting out as an off-shift computer operator and currently I am a second-line manager.

Although I show a cross on the past branch, that doesn't mean my faith is not important to me today—it's just that I used to be heavily involved in church (teaching Sunday School as well as being a church administrator and treasurer for more than a decade).

My greatest failure was my marriage (two rings). I've been involved in a divorce that has been going on for 2 years now. As I've told others, this isn't something I would wish on my worst enemy. As I'll note later, my family views me as the stable one—the one who never changes and makes all the right and moral decisions. This major life event has me on a rollercoaster [sic] of emotion—one that I can't get off of because it seems that this will keep going on forever.

Working backwards on the "state" branch, I've lived in Rochester, Minnesota, for my adult life. I attended high school in Spring Valley, Minnesota, which is only 20 minutes from Rochester. I did spend some time with my mother in New Or-

leans (junior in high school). This hurricane season has hit home for me [not only] in seeing the pictures, but also not hearing yet from two cousins. My family spent 1 year in Chicago; however, most of my childhood was spent in Ellington, New York (born in New York as well). Although Ellington is a very small town, it supported the town kids in sports enthusiastically. My favorite was baseball. As a catcher, my goal was to make the traveling team (baseball and smiley face)—which did happen.

My father is connected to two branches—Family and The Past. When I turned 16, my parents divorced. It was at that time that he told me that he never wanted a son at all and wished I had not been born. I wasn't upset mainly because he had not spent much time with me growing up, so it's hard to know what you're missing when you didn't have it to begin with. Now that he is getting older and his health is deteriorating, he is making attempts to talk with me—I'm just not sure if I want to yet. There is a lot of distance (winding black branch) that I'm not sure can be overcome.

Family

When my father left us, my mother told me I needed to get a job and help her support my two sisters. My sisters are twins and they are 5 years younger than I. Although I was too young to see it at the time, I became the "man of the house," and having to assume so much responsibility so young (I was paying the majority of the bills), I ended up becoming like a superhero (the Superman logo). Ironically, I would later come to shun this stereotype and persona—for I was held on a pedestal others would not let me come down from. It took my standing up and adamantly stating that I didn't have all the answers and that I am just as human as anyone else, before they saw that I had changed and would no longer "play the part."

Unfortunately, one of my sisters suffered a heart attack this past year. She came through it okay, but events such as this make one seriously look at their own life, family, health, and even the words we say (or don't) to others.

I have several nieces and nephews that I care for deeply and wish we could be closer.

4 Me

Three years ago I went through a mid-life crisis (my second life event). I describe my experience as:

1. *Unscrew the top off Mike's head.*
2. *Pull out Mike's brain.*
3. *Put someone else's brain back in (a random brain will do nicely).*
4. *Screw the top back on.*
5. *Say the words "Scoot. Off you go."*
6. *Let's see what happens to the lab experiment.*

One day I woke up and everything I liked to do, such as reading, my job, watching sports, etc., etc—I didn't like anymore. I felt foreign. So I got on a treadmill. This also coincided with my mother having a heart attack. I was extremely overweight and when I went in to have myself checked out, in a span of 4 hours I had gone from seeing my family doctor to a top heart specialist at Mayo. Given my health and lifestyle, he gave me

Figure 10.5 (left) "Before" photo
Figure 10.6 (right) Current photo

5 years to live. In the course of a year from the time I got on the treadmill, I lost 130 pounds (running shoe, me before and after). Call it anger, angst, or even rage—that was my motivation. I ran from 2–5 miles a day, every day. Above are a couple of before and after pictures.

It's funny to me that although I've always been a "Type A" personality, I now often find myself sitting on my balcony watching sunsets (the road leading to the hills with the sun setting behind). The simple things in life seem to appeal to me more than ever before.

Although it led to my weight gain earlier in life, I found I had a knack for cooking (fork, spoon, and knife). Although it may have to wait until I retire, I would like to attend a chef-training school to see how far I could take that skill.

Finally, although I could have put it under hobbies, I do on occasion write some poetry—it helps me to collect my thoughts. I put it here because there are very few people I would show this to, so for the most part it really is just "4 Me."

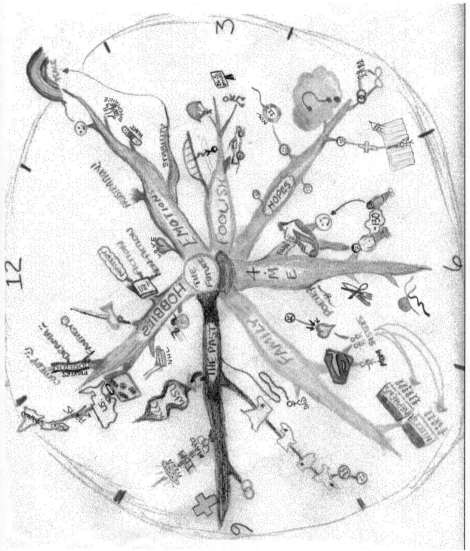

Figure 10.7 The Future

IDEA MAPPING

Hopes

My hopes are all about the future and most are unknown (the question mark in the cloud). I included lots of smiley faces as I wish for the best.

I do want to be in a relationship sometime in the future (two more rings). I also hope to have a family and that it will last forever (infinity symbol).

These past 2 years I've been searching again for the meaning of my life. There have been many, many days I question what good I am. Ironically, in November 2004, I got an answer for at least 1 day. I was in my office wondering this very question when my door burst open. One of my administrative assistants ran in with her arms waving and unable to talk—I didn't have a clue at first of what was happening. She had enough sense to spin around and put my hand in front of her stomach—she was choking on a piece of food. I almost had someone die in my arms that day. After four tries, she started to slump forward in my arms. On the fifth try, I thought for sure I was going to hurt her, but fortunately it was on that final try that the food dislodged and she took a gasp of air. Although we don't talk about it much, we have a bond that can never be broken. That was Veteran's Day (November 11— life preserver). Although it was a very good thing, I can see where I tend to erase the positive, focus more on what I could/should be doing, and then become down as I try to jump-start myself once more to other things.

I do attend church again but, for the most part, stay on the fringe (smaller cross). Although I want to take things more slowly than in the past, I was asked to play a role in a drama in the near future (me on stage).

Foolish

Every once in a while I tend to do something crazy (e.g., driving a car at 150 mph). Most of these I haven't done yet as my family members try to talk me out of them—maybe it's a good thing they do. I've threatened to go bungee jumping off a bridge or go parachuting quite often. I am thinking of training for a marathon. This past July I ran my first 5k race. All of the proceeds went to one of my coworkers who has been battling brain cancer for the past 10 months. His initial prognosis was 18 months to live and when I crossed the finish line, he met me there. I whispered to him that I would run that race every year if he would continue to meet me at the finish line. He is one of my heroes.

Emotions

Most of my life I've kept my emotions buried (part of my upbringing). The branch is primarily red and it actually turned into a vein which burst open when I thought of all the frustration I've experienced by not letting my feelings (like love) show. The stability branch is in gold, as it is what several seem to prize the most in life. That branch leads to peace (the rainbow). However, most people (including me) are unable to take the easy path, so they have to go through hurt (bandage) and come to a point of acceptance (open hands) before they can be happy and hopefully peaceful.

Conclusion

After I had drawn all of this, I somehow felt that my future had boundaries or limitations and yet I didn't know how to show that. Then I got the idea for the clock. When I consider that I am over 40, I realize that I can still do much in life but it is an eventual march against time. Finally, although I had no clue I had done this when I drew the clock, I found it interesting that "peace falls outside time." There is a lesson in there somewhere.

World Trade Center Memorial Park

Kaizad Irani is an architect who left the corporate world because of his passion to teach—and he is one of the best at it! Kaizad is currently a professor of landscape architecture with Parkland College in Champaign, Illinois. He is a sought-after guest professor by universities all over the world. I count it a privilege to know him. Below is the story about his map. Refer to Figure 10.8.

Two years after the tragic events of September 11, 2001, the city of New York started looking at various memorials to help the residents and the world heal from the aftermath of devastation. They contacted the Associated Landscape Contractors of America (ALCA), and initiated a design competition to create a landscape design for a memorial park that would be built in Lower Manhattan under the shadow of Ground Zero.

In May, 2003, the finalists (including myself) for the design charrette met in Chicago and started working on the landscape plan. The design charrette consisted of approximately 30 finalists who were some of the top landscape architects and designers in the country. Each architect was assigned to one of five teams, and the teams were given 2 days to come up with a landscape plan for the WTC (World Trade Center)

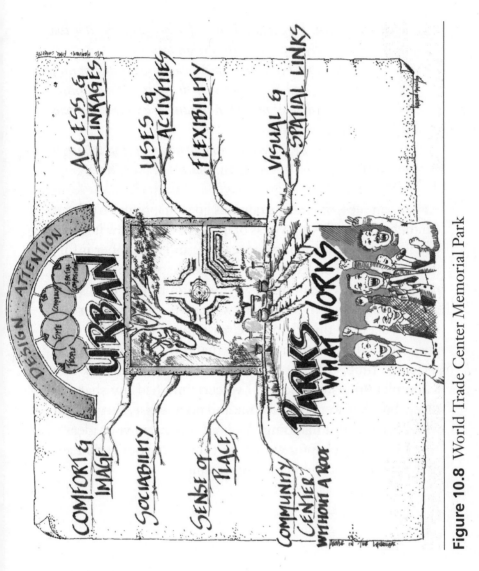

Figure 10.8 World Trade Center Memorial Park

Memorial Park. I created this map for my team during the initial Site Analysis phase of the design process.

The map that I created helped explain to the design jury the significance and importance of designing the winning project. It showed what makes an urban park work. This was a key aspect to our success.

Currently, the project [is] undergoing some final changes and logistical issues before its installation in New York.

As you can see from these examples, idea mapping isn't about a bunch of rules. It's a process of understanding how it is that our brains associate, collect, organize, and remember information and then of deciding on the best way to represent and use that data in a meaningful way. See Figure 10.9 for a summary of the different idea maps where we saw how the rules were broken in this chapter. Create maps that fulfill your purposes and create them in a way that is visually pleasing. At the same time, feel free to create idea maps that look like a complete disaster. I know I've certainly had my share of those, but they were only for me and no one else. Be yourself when you are idea mapping. After all—they are your ideas!

In the next chapter we will revisit one of your earlier activities and see how you are progressing.

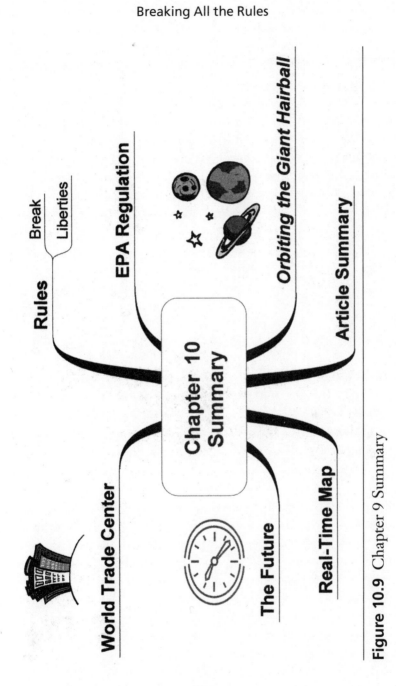

Figure 10.9 Chapter 9 Summary

11

Your Presentation Revisited

I n this chapter, you will do the following:

- Recreate your first activity from Chapter 2—only this time you'll use an idea map.
- Compare your baseline note-taking attempt to your new idea-mapping skills.
- Review the benefits of mapping a presentation.

In Chapter 2, before learning to idea map, you chose a topic for a 30-minute presentation, created the notes that you would take to the podium, and created them in your usual format. I called these notes your baseline notes. The purpose of this activity was to make you aware of your current note-taking style. We are going to do this activity again, only this time it will be done by using your idea-mapping skills. You will then compare your initial baseline notes with the idea map you will create in this next activity.

Presentation—Second Attempt

One of the struggles in the original activity was choosing a topic that you could talk about for 30 minutes. You can reuse this same topic or choose a new one. If you don't have a presentation theme in mind, take a moment to create a small idea map of possible topics. Next, decide on one of the topics and take 5 minutes to create the notes you will take to the podium using your new idea-mapping technique. The objectives are speed (pretend you're under a deadline) and volume of data. Let the thoughts come naturally and randomly. Get them down as quickly as you can. Don't worry about changing colors or being neat. At the end of the 5 minutes, assign each main branch a number to determine the order and sequence of the presentation.

Now find your baseline notes from Chapter 2. When comparing this map to your original notes, ask yourself the following questions:

1. Did I struggle as much in choosing a topic?
2. Did I have a greater number of topics to choose from?
3. Which document contains a greater amount of information?
4. Which one is more organized?
5. Could I give a presentation from this idea map?
6. Were there any images in the map?
7. Which one looks messier? (Probably the idea map!)

Benefits of Presentation Maps

As you will discover if you use this map to deliver an actual presentation, there are a number of benefits for using the map for delivery purposes. For example:

- It gives you flexibility to adjust the order of or the importance placed on a branch at the last moment. Maybe when you arrive for your meeting you find out that a particular part of your presentation is critical to the audience.

- It gives you the ability to take the same basic topics and adjust it to fit the needs and applications of different audiences.

- It gives you the ability to adjust the time. This is the infamous original "20-minute" presentation that must now be done in 10 minutes because some previous presenter talked for too long!!

- It gives you the ability to read your audience as you present, because you can look at them (rather than your notes!). In addition you eliminate both the visual and the audible distraction of shuffling through multiple pieces of paper.

- It gives you a chance to express yourself more naturally because you are looking at key thoughts. Most people using linear notes sound like they are reading a from script—and they are!

Next time you have an opportunity to speak to a group, use an idea map. See Figure 11.1 for a map of the benefits for using an idea map as opposed to using baseline notes.

Chapter 12 will provide you with many choices of idea-mapping applications—allowing you to practice your skills!

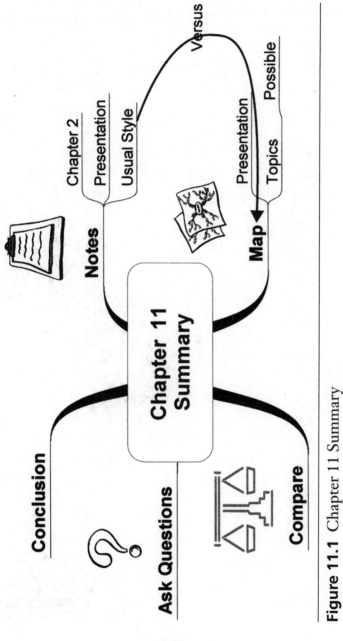

Figure 11.1 Chapter 11 Summary

12

Idea-Mapping Menu

The following menu of selections is a series of idea-mapping applications and suggested practice activities. The various topics include:

1. To-Do List
2. Decision
3. Keeping a Journal
4. Personal Planning
5. Vision or Mission
6. Goals
7. Client
8. Project Plan
9. Problem
10. Book
11. Preparing and Delivering a Presentation
12. Article
13. A Person
14. Phone Calls
15. Job or Process Description
16. Gift
17. Writing a Document
18. Status Report
19. Team Idea Map
20. Study Notes
21. In-Box
22. "Real-Time" Notes
23. Interview
24. Capturing Notes During a Group Meeting

25. Designing a Website
26. Memorizing Information
27. Teaching Someone to Map
28. Organizing Your Thoughts

Try these maps in any order you prefer and commit to doing at least one new application per week. This will help to solidify your mapping skills. Try both hand drawing as well as using software products to create the maps.

1. To-Do List

Creating a "to-do" list in the idea-mapping format provides a fun and creative look at tasks. It can help categorize similar items and assist in prioritizing. This is a simple way to practice. Some people will argue that it takes longer to create a to-do map than it does just writing a normal list—especially during the early learning phase. This may be true. However, mapping something familiar will get the focus off struggling with content and further enable you to focus your energy on learning to structure thoughts by association.

People frequently ask me how to "check off" the completed items. Do this by putting a small box at the end of each branch. As items are finished, check the box. I redraw the idea map when it reaches the point where it is difficult to add new branches or it is just so messy I can't stand it any more.

2. Decision

Making decisions can often occupy our minds as we wrestle with all the possibilities. Try creating a map that shows all the issues affecting the decision. What are the key factors to consider? What are all the alternatives? Does this decision impact others? What will be the result of making the decision? Are there financial implications? Who could provide advice? What are the positive, negative, and interesting thoughts that come to mind? Sometimes seeing the whole picture will spark an idea that previously went unnoticed. Documenting all the issues might even help you sleep better!

3. Keeping a Journal

A number of my workshop participants have changed how they journal. Instead of using lined paper, purchase a sketchpad with unlined paper, making sure that the paper thickness is above average. This will keep markers from bleeding through the paper. Create an idea map for each of the entries. Linear notes can be included on the opposite page, if necessary.

4. Personal Planning—Wedding, Party, Holiday Event, Shopping, Vacation

Idea maps are a great tool for any type of planning—from huge weddings to Christmas shopping trips! They are great for planning big events and family vacations. I've seen grocery maps that use the store aisles as main branches and others organized by food group—dairy, meats, cereal, fruit, vegetables, household, and canned goods.

Planning with idea maps is a great way to get others involved in the process. Keep them posted where others can see them and add their ideas.

5. Vision or Mission—
Individual or Organizational

In Chapter 6, I suggested creating a personal vision or mission. This can be so valuable that it is worth repeating. However, this one may be a work in progress, so remain patient.

The same idea applies for a group of people working toward a shared objective. The creation of the central image alone will bring clarity to the purpose and vision. Each person will see how he or she fits into the overall picture and will have a better understanding of the organizational direction. The vision defined in these maps can cover the corporate strategic plan, a 1-year vision, or a short-term project. Too often professionals spend enormous amounts of time working in isolation on their part of a project while the entire team shares little communication. Taking a short amount of time with the entire group to create this vision will save time, money, and frustration. It will increase buy-in, understanding, and interdependence among the team members.

6. Goals

Goals are different from vision. Goals are what you want to accomplish at the detail level. Goals are how you intend to achieve the set vision. Some people traditionally set goals (resolutions) every New Year. New goals are set after an annual performance review. Maybe it's easier to set monthly or weekly goals. This is a personal choice. Just set them and map them. It significantly increases the chances of successful completion.

A goal map is a beautiful visual reminder of priorities. It

keeps the creator from becoming distracted by unimportant issues. These maps can also be documentation for past accomplishments.

7. Client

This is another large category of possible maps. Various topics could include client meetings, proposals, products, issues, presentations, business growth, or just a map of personnel (names, roles, responsibilities, and other notable details about each person). Years ago, the owners of a Pennsylvania consulting company attended my workshop. They returned for a visit the following year and brought some of their maps with them. One was a spiral bound document with an idea map as the front cover. It was a client proposal. The map cover summarized the entire contents of the proposal including research, requirements gathering, and recommendations. In the subsequent text of the document were all the linear details. It was the best of both worlds, but you can probably guess what immediately captured the client's attention!

By using idea maps with clients, you will stand apart from the competition by communicating with the customer in a visual and memorable way. Caution: If you are taking live notes in front of someone (customer or anyone else) not familiar with idea mapping, explain what you are doing or it may be distracting—especially if you come armed with all of your markers!

8. Project Plan

Try creating a map to track all the key components of a project. This will assist the entire project team by providing a visual reminder of upcoming deadlines, task priorities, problem areas, budget, and client information, to name just a few possibilities. Mindjet software would be another option for handling large amounts of data, and it can export the map to and from Microsoft Project, if applicable.

It is in some of these more complex applications that you begin to experience the tremendous power, clarity, and timesavings you can gain by having a tool to house all the data in one place. Use the map to share the project status with others or during meetings.

9. Problem

Choose a current problem to map. Include all aspects of the problem and a branch for possible alternatives. When did this problem start? What is the root cause of the problem? What would it take to resolve the issue? Are there any deadlines to consider? Document the individuals involved in this problem, their roles, and contributions to the solution. What are the worst- and best-case scenarios? Often what you thought was the problem ends up being a symptom and the map lets the underlying cause be seen more clearly—and of course the possible solutions will be more effective.

10. Book

How often do you read a book, then go back and try to find a piece of information that you need but can't find? Putting all the key pieces of data from a book onto a single map remedies this problem. In addition, it presents a perfect way to review the material. Organize the idea map by chapter or define other categories. Add page numbers to the branches to assist in referring to important sections of the book.

I've seen detailed book maps on flipchart paper and smaller idea maps copied right into the front of the book where there are typically two blank pages. The next time you read a book, keep an idea map to track your major thoughts and learning.

11. Preparing and Delivering a Presentation

Mapping a presentation is a wonderful application. I use this application multiple times a month. It is fabulous for collecting, organizing, and prioritizing topics. It may take more than one draft to get it right, but once it is complete you can speak from the map. The delivery will be much smoother and more natural compared to other presenters who must shuffle through pages and pages of linear notes.

Don Lacombe was a course participant and a 30+ year veteran (now retired) of one of the largest automotive companies. Using the Mindjet software, he created a large map to present complex data to the executives of a sister company. The data covered 5 years of research on a competitor. He gave an $11'' \times 17''$ version of this map to each of his attendees.

Part way through, his presentation was interrupted to allow time for another presenter. This person finished delivering his information, and then it was Don's turn again. Using his map, he did a quick recap of what he had covered prior to the interruption and then finished the presentation. It was a smashing success! He later used the same map to give many internal presentations and still uses it periodically for his own purposes today.

12. Article

Find an article that you need to read. Start by scanning the article for themes or main ideas. If it is easy to identify the main branches, do that much of the map before reading the article. Otherwise, determine possible main branches while reading the article.

People often ask whether they should read the whole article first and create the map afterwards or create the map as they read. It's completely a personal choice. The one thing I definitely recommend is that you highlight key words as you read. That way if you read the entire article prior to creating the map, the potential key words are already there even if they do not all go into the map. This eliminates the need to reread the article. Remember—only capture the key words needed to support the defined purpose and the words or images you will need to remember.

13. A Person

There are many opportunities to create what I call people maps. The person can be real or imaginary, living or deceased. The map could describe a client you want to remember, a job candidate, a sales contact, a family member, a historical or prominent figure, your ideal future spouse, a mentor, or YOU! There are millions of people to choose from.

Begin by defining your purpose because it's tempting to include too many details on this one! Some data will probably be similar in all people maps. Those items make up the essence of your relationship with that individual. Although this is an incomplete list, consider including some of the following information about the person when creating this map:

Hobbies
Where does and has this person lived?
Memories
Talents
Awards
Shared experiences
Dreams
Favorites (foods, destinations, colors)
How did you meet?
Education
Common interests
Friends
Work
Family
Personality
Activity involvement
Passions
Future plans together

Use your imagination to go wild with the possibilities. Enjoy!

14. Phone Calls

For this application, create a phone map prior to making a call. This will help focus the discussion and make sure all pertinent issues are covered. As the conversation takes place, add action items, decisions, and any follow-up tasks to the map. The central image could be a combination of the person you are calling and the date. If necessary, keep a binder to store and document these conversations.

15. Job or Process Description (Book of Knowledge)

Practice idea mapping by documenting your job. Try to cover every aspect as if this document could assist you in training a replacement. It will be eye opening to discover the vastness and complexity of responsibilities.

Dan Drayton worked as a supplier quality specialist for a large automotive company. His assignment was to create a map for his specific commodity—bumper systems. The intention of the exercise was to help his boss understand the processes and complexity involved in the fabrication of a number of commodities. It would establish a book of knowledge and assist in understanding the product's process flow.

Dan's specific commodity, bumper systems, contained many additional processes that were unique to this product (polishing, chroming, painting, as well as impact performance and warranty issues). He created a map that contained all the different processes, systems, and key elements that were critical in manufacturing a complete bumper system. The map simplified and organized his thoughts, distinguished each process, and created a semblance of order from a confusing and complicated process flow. He was also able to use it as a problem solving and root-cause analysis tool.

His idea map started out as a job description and grew to a living, breathing document. The map was updated as the processes changed. No more reinventing the wheel! Create a map of your job.

16. Gift

Here are some gift ideas:

- A map of a person given to that individual (see the description of making a PERSON map earlier in this chapter)
- A map of a presentation given to the presenter
- Cards—birthday, holiday, thank you, and so on
- A map of an author's book or article given to the author—(that is *not* a hint!)

I once had a client who was retiring from Chevrolet. An artist created a map of his history with the company, his hobby (fishing), his family, and other details about his life. He received it as a retirement gift.

While getting into my car after work one day, I noticed a huge basket of fruit in the passenger's seat. My first thought was, "who broke into my car?" Amidst all of the fruit was an idea map titled, "The Fruits of the Spirit." My husband had created a map to brighten my day and left it as a gift. It is one of the sweetest gifts I have ever received.

17. Writing a Document

I can't think of a better way to collect and organize thoughts before writing any kind of document. Remind yourself to let the ideas come naturally. Don't get stuck feeling as if they need to be captured sequentially. Once you've captured all the ideas, decide on their order. This map will be a draft and often never gets redrawn. From here you can create the linear document. If there is value added, include a final draft of the idea map with the linear document. You will be pleased with the organization, the flow, and the speed at which you were able to create the final product.

Consider developing a report, a proposal, a meeting summary, a white paper, a contract, a BLOG, or a lessons-learned document using this technique.

18. Status Report

Build a status map by adding information to a map over time. Create a template of the major branches that you use every week or month. Leave a miscellaneous branch for the unique events during each period. When it's time to write the report, it's all there! Keep the map as a historical collection of accomplishments as described in one of the examples in Chapter 6. Consider including the map with the linear document, but don't turn in the map by itself unless you are willing to explain the new format and its contents to the recipient.

19. Team Mapping Process

See Chapter 9 for a description of this application. Gather a bunch of markers and give it a try!

20. Study Notes

Whether it is getting a degree, taking a single class, learning something new for the job, or earning a certification—it all requires studying. Creating an idea map that includes new information will speed up and enhance the learning process and make the data more memorable. You can create a map that covers a chapter, a lecture, or the entire subject. It's up to you. If possible, post it on your office wall as a way to review the material. It will make learning easier.

21. In-Box

One of the most discouraging things I hear professionals talk about is the vast amount of information that piles into both their physical and electronic in-boxes. Try creating a mail map to collect pertinent information, and then delete the mail! Scan each message or document for information you need to remember. Create a branch for the information or add to a previous one. Do this for each in-box message and then post the map for review. What an easy way to keep the necessary bits of information, without keeping the entire message or article.

22. Real-Time Notes

This is the most challenging idea-mapping activity. For a complete description on how to be successful at this application, see Chapter 13.

23. Interview

This map could be your preparation for conducting an interview, taking notes as the interview is in process, or both. In preparing for an interview, create branches for each topic you want to cover. Use colors, symbols, or numbers to prioritize critical information. Take this map to the interview and add to it as the questions are answered.

For taking notes during an interview, refer to the suggestions under the "Real-Time Notes" category.

24. Capturing Notes During a Group Meeting

This is "real-time" mapping on steroids. Now the map isn't just for your purposes, it's for the group and will help to facilitate the progress of the meeting. Have you ever been in a meeting where people repeatedly bring up the same issues? Try capturing the important discussion points from a meeting in an idea map. Use a flipchart, whiteboard, or software to house the data. Keep it visible for all to see throughout the meeting. If discussions become repetitive, you can point to that part of the map and ask if they have thoughts in addition to those already discussed. People will even begin to tell you where to put their thoughts on the map.

Occasionally individuals will disagree about where a new subtopic connects on the map. This is a great opportunity to further clarify understanding and then mutually agree on its placement. You can then distribute the map to all in attendance since it was a shared creation.

25. Designing a Website

A website is much like an idea map. The home page houses the connections to all the main links. If you are developing a website, start collecting possible ideas for your site in a map. It's best to use the software for this activity because you can then easily export your map to an html file and have the guts of the work already completed! One of my clients, The Chattanooga Advertising Federation, used a map to communicate changes on their current site to the web designers. They were told that their up-front work saved them $1,100.

26. Memorizing Information

If you need to memorize the information in the map, put as many images into the map as possible. Use codes and color to help trigger your recall. Do a mental review within an hour of creating the map, and see how much you can recall without peeking. Once you have gone through that exercise, check your accuracy by reviewing the actual map. Do this again 24 hours later, 1 week later, and 1 month later. This process moves the information from your short-term memory to your long-term memory. Post it where it is visible if that is helpful.

27. Teaching Someone to Map

There is no better way to reinforce your learning than by teaching idea mapping to someone else. Show them one of yours. Explain the benefits and a bit about the map. Find an application that would be both useful and simple for them to try. Maybe you can do one together.

28. Organizing Your Thoughts

This is a very simple—yet extremely useful—application. Have you ever experienced a time when your thoughts just seemed to go in circles and finding a good starting point seemed very difficult? Purge your brain by pouring all the (sometimes seemingly unrelated) items onto a map. This has many advantages. First, your head feels less full! Next, you can look at what is on the map and decide on the priorities or the urgent items. You can take control. Now it is possible to decide what to attack first, and you can think more clearly.

In all of the previous chapters, I provided a chapter summary. This one is a little different—you create your own review. Choose several applications from this chapter that you would like to map. Use those as the main branches of the map in Figure 12.1. You will have your own summary and plan of action!

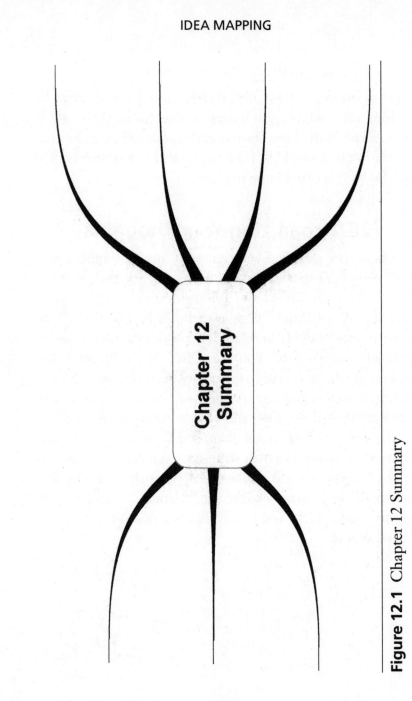

Figure 12.1 Chapter 12 Summary

13

Real-Time Idea Mapping—The Final Challenge

This chapter will cover

- The Definition of Real-Time Idea Mapping
- The Five Keys to Successful Real-Time Idea Mapping

The Definition of Real-Time Idea Mapping

Real-time idea mapping is creating your map while the information is coming at you in the moment. It combines everything you know about listening, making decisions on the amount of detail to include, boiling thoughts into key words, using images to represent large portions of data or to enhance recall, and deciding on your purpose for the map.

The watermark on the cover of this book was a real-time map that I created in 1998 in front of a large audience during a 3-hour presentation. Talk about pressure! I captured the main points of the speaker's message even when there were parts I didn't completely understand. You also saw an example from Choon Boo Lim in Chapter 10.

This is the most challenging idea-mapping activity. Tackle this after you have some experience with other mapping applications. In a "real-time" note-taking situation (such as a lecture), there can be many challenges present at the same time, including:

- High speed of delivery
- No agenda provided
- Difficulty managing your markers
- Frustration
- Lack of defined purpose
- Disorganized presenter or facilitator
- Boring presenter or facilitator
- Hard to determine main branches and key words
- Desire to change back to linear notes
- Running out of space on the paper

First a note of encouragement—this is an advanced application, and it will take a variety of attempts to feel comfortable, so be persistent! Given all of these challenges, let me make a few key suggestions.

The Five Keys to Successful Real-Time Idea Mapping

1. Start Small

Make sure you are comfortable with idea mapping before using it in critical or difficult scenarios. In the 2-day course I teach, participants face a challenging activity like this on the afternoon of the second day. Even with their thorough training, I suggest they begin with small and safe "real-time" applications.

Start with a situation in which the sharing of information happens at a relatively reasonable speed—a meeting for example. The pace is slower because discussions can get repetitive, there is usually an agenda, and sometimes (dare I say) they can be boring. This provides an opportunity to focus on trying the mapping technique and preventing boredom at the same time. Your notes will end up being more complete, succinct, and organized than anyone else's in the room. Mapping the meeting will keep you engaged and provide an opportunity to hone your skills at the same time! Tell the group what you are doing so you don't become a distraction by "doodling" through the meeting. Everyone will want to see the map at the end of the meeting.

2. Purpose

Define your purpose for taking notes. This will guide what information is included in the map and the amount of detail.

3. Pre-Draw Main Branches

If possible, pre-draw the main branches. You might find these on an agenda, they could comprise your previous knowledge about the topic, or they might summarize what you would like to gain from the map. Even if there is an agenda, this is no guarantee the speaker will follow it. Your job is to keep your ears and mind keenly attuned to the main and key ideas that are important to YOU. These will become the main branches and detail branches of your map. When examining the map afterward, don't worry if in hindsight you decide you want to change its organization. If the first map has served its purpose, stop there. However, if there is a reason, you can make updates later in a second draft.

4. Challenge Yourself

As you tackle more challenging "real-time" applications, the issues and difficulties you will face will include: greater volumes of information coming at you with an increased rate of speed, greater complexity of the information, and disorganized information. With higher speeds, I recommend sticking to a single color or using a four-color pen (click quietly). Don't waste time switching marker colors. If you run out of space on your paper, start a second sheet with the same central image and off you go! With greater complexity—just do your best to catch the highlights. Fill in the necessary details later.

If you find you are dealing with a disorganized speaker who switches back and forth between topics, add new information to the branch that seems most appropriate. If the facilitator repeats thoughts multiple times, resist adding the repetitive information to the map unless there is a purpose. Use arrows or symbols to show connections and repetition if it is helpful. Stay alert.

As you get comfortable, try longer and more complicated events. Tackle a presentation in which there is no agenda provided. I'll bet your idea map will end up being more organized than the speaker's presentation!

5. Stick With It!!!

Try to avoid frustration. Don't give up!! Taking notes in this format almost guarantees capturing more data than linear notes. Yes, it might look like a total mess, but you will be able to understand it because it is your creation. The next time it will be so much easier.

Meetings, sermons, presentations, conference speeches, and videos provide opportunities to practice this advanced skill. Give it a try. See Figure 13.1 for a summary of this chapter.

Conclusion

We have finally arrived at the end of this book. Have you begun to get a glimpse of your hidden brain power? Have idea maps already helped you to learn, plan, think, or create faster in any way? Have you enjoyed the process so far? Do you see how idea maps can be a tool to achieve greater success in business and life? If you answer yes to any of these questions, you are well into this adventure.

My final charge to you is this—Practice! Although this is still a new skill, you should feel a great sense of accomplishment in seeing such progress. It truly is a process. Each person is going to grow their idea-mapping skills at different speeds. Some will use this tool for complex issues while others will use it for more simple purposes. Remember, the measure of success isn't the beauty of the map. Most of the examples in this book look much more spectacular than the majority of my own creations. The measure of success is in finding, learning, and using a tool that will lead you to new ways of thinking. I measure my personal success by the degree to which this tool helps you. I hope that the use of idea mapping will make your work and life more productive, creative, memorable, fun, clear, abundant, organized, imaginative, colorful, and filled with possibilities!

Allow yourself to embrace and enjoy this new way of thinking, learning, and creating. Give yourself this gift. You have nothing to lose and everything to gain. I hope it enriches your work and life as much as it has mine. Now get out there and start idea mapping with a vengeance!

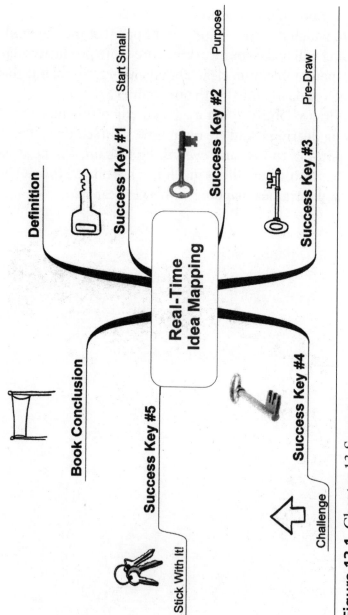

Figure 13.1 Chapter 13 Summary

Appendix 1
Summary of Lessons

Lesson One—Define your purpose for taking notes.

Lesson Two—Where your brain goes, you will follow.

Lesson Three—Two individuals' idea maps on an identical topic will look different.

Lesson Four—Just capture ideas. Order comes later.

Lesson Five—Starting position: Follow the laws—for now.

Lesson Six—Use key words, identify main branches versus subbranches, and learn to draw simple icons.

Lesson Seven—A single key word generates more thoughts than a phrase.

Lesson Eight—Get ideas for idea-mapping applications by seeing others' examples.

Lesson Nine—Try using software.

Lesson Ten—Be patient with yourself. You're learning a new skill!

Lesson Eleven—Clearly identify a single, simple, and specific topic for the Team Mapping Method.

Lesson Twelve—Always start the team mapping process by asking each participant to create an individual map around the defined topic.

Appendix 2
More Information

For more information on idea-mapping, workshops, and certifications see the following resources:

NastGroup, Inc.
Website: www.IdeaMappingSuccess.com
Email: info@IdeaMappingSuccess.com
Blog: http://ideamapping.blogspot.com/
Phone within the United States: 866-896-1024 toll free
Phone outside of the United States: 734-207-5287

NastGroup, Inc. partner *The Learning Consortium* in the UK
Phone: +44(0) 1202 674676
Website: www.ThinkLearnCreateAndLive.com

NastGroup, Inc. now offers a new product called an ***Idea Mapping Kit***. This 7$\frac{1}{16}$" × 9$\frac{1}{8}$" 3-ring binder comes with 10 fine-tip markers, paper, a 3-hole punched zipper case, a business card holder, and a 4-color pen. For information on how to purchase your Idea Mapping Kit, go to http://IdeaMappingSuccess.com/IMKit.cfm.

Index

Accomplishments, examples of branches and, 86, 89
Action items, lack of organization and, 46–47
Activity involvement, 238
Age, 178
Alexander, Jeff, 102–104
American Bankers Association (ABA), xiv, 2, 171
Antianemia drugs, 157–158
Antianginals, 159, 161, 162
Antihistamines, 155–156
Antihypertensives, 159, 160
Article mapping, 230, 237
Associated Landscape Contractors of America (ALCA), 218
Association, branches and, 42. *See also* Blooming; Flowing
Association of Christian Schools International, xiv, 2
Associative thinking, 27–29
Audience, reading the, 226
Authors, key words, 66

Balance, visual, 44
Baseline notes, 26
  adding images to, 56, 58
  determining key words and, 52
  explained, 12–13
  identifying main branches and, 54, 56
Bess, Dave, 112
Bess, Judy, 109–112
Biondo, Dario, 113

BLOG, 241
Blooming, 27–29
  branches and, 42
  combining methods, 30
  vs. flowing, 32
  team mapping process and, 185
BMC Software, xiv, 2
Book mapping, 230, 236
Book titles, key words and, 66
BP, xiv, 2
BP Cherry Point Refinery, 139
BrainBloom, 27–29, 94, 115, 185
Brain activity, learning and, 14
Brain capacity, exploring, 36
Branches:
  main, 40–43
    identifying, 53–54, 55, 58
    obstacles and, 74
  subbranches, 41, 54, 58, 74
Budget, 122
Bullet points key words and, 63
Bumper systems, 239
Buzan, Tony, xvi, 20, 78
Buzan Organization, xiii, xviii, 7–8, 24, 92, 104

Cahill, Michael, 23
Cancer, 109–112
Central image:
  balance and, 44
  line connections and, 68, 70
  as an obstacle, 78
Chattanooga Advertising Federation, 244

Chemical warfare, 153–154
Chief Knowledge Officer (CKO), 141,
   143–146
Chronology. *See* Sequential order
Clarity Creative Group, 105
Clark, Megan, 199–202
Client mapping, 230, 234
Clustering, 176
Codes, central image and, 40
Cold calls, 134, 135. *See also* Phone calls
Color, 13, 22, 73
   branches and, 41
   central image and, 40
   drawing icons and, 56
   laws of idea mapping and, 37
Coloring books, 56
Comic strips, 56
Communication, 15
Company logo, 56
Company stability, 122
Conflicts, examples of branches and,
   86, 88
Confusion, untrained brains and, 14
ConocoPhillips, xiv, 2
Consolidations, 187–189
Core, dual, 105, 108, 109
Cortical skills, 2
Covey, Steven, xiii, 7–9, 95
Creativity, 13, 15
   barriers to, 26
Customer support, 122

Dancing With Brilliance, 113
Data:
   managing large volumes of, 124–125
   volume and complexity, 122
Decision making, 15
   maps, 230, 231–232
Definitions, key words and, 66
Detail:
   level of, as an obstacle, 75
   note taking and, 13
Diagrams, key words and, 66
Diesel Blending Project SPA, 197
Dietrich, Sandy, 203
Dimension, branches and, 41–42

Discussion, difficult, 100–101
Document, writing a, 230, 241
Drafting, obstacles to, 75–77
Drayton, Dan, 239
Dreams, 238
DTE Energy, xiv, 2
Duryea, Trygve, 141, 143–146
The Dwight School, xiv, 2

Edison, Thomas, 50–51
Education, 175–176, 238
Electronic Data Systems, xiii, 3, 6
Employee, problem, 100–101
Employment, 238
   description, 230, 239–240
   performance, 15
   review, data collection for annual, 85–89
Environment of fun, 186
Environmental Protection Agency (EPA)
   regulation, 197–199
Estate planning, 89–100
Evacuation plans, 178
Expenses, examples of branches and, 86,
   88–89

Financial goals, examples of branches
   and, 86
Fiscal Year, 141–146
Flexibility:
   loss of, 126
   presentation maps and, 225
Flowing, 28–29
   vs. blooming, 32
   branches and, 42
   combining methods, 30
Ford Motor Company, xiv, 2
Franklin Templeton, xiv, 2

General Motors, xiv, 2
Get Ahead, 105
Gift mapping, 230, 240
Goal mapping, 230, 233–234
Goleman, Daniel, 100
Grade point average (GPA), 178
Grow, Carey, 171–174
Guidelines. *See* Idea mapping, laws of

Index

Hagwood, Scott, 126
Hallmark, 200
Hayes, Kirsty, 113, 114
Hewlett-Packard, linear communication
    and, 1
Hierarchy, branches and, 42
Highlighters:
    central image and, 37, 40
    determining categories and, 54
History and Uses of Graphical Lang-
    uages, 23
Hobbies, 209–210, 238
Holiday events, 230, 232
Humor, central image and, 40
Hurricane Wilma, 178

IBM, 211
Icons, 45
    drawing simple, 56–58
    preloaded, 122
Idea generation, 79–80
Idea mapping:
    benefits of, 14–16
    creating, 47–48
Idea mapping (*continued*):
    definition, 20–21
    developing, 43–47
    large, 104–105, 106–107
    laws of, 36–37 (*see also specific type*)
    learning by example, 84–85 (*see also*
        specific type)
    lessons, summary of, 255
    linear thinking and, 2
    menu, 230, 246 (*see also specific type*)
    as a natural process, 12
    read, how to, 37–43
    rules of, breaking, 196–197, 211
    three basic skills, 50–60
    workshop information, 256
Images:
    central, 37, 40
        main branches and, 40
    fear of drawing, 124
    laws of idea mapping and, 37
    as an obstacle, 78
    preloaded, 122

use of, 13
Imagination, 13
In-box mapping, 230, 242
Individualization, rule breaking and,
    196–197, 211
Information:
    representation of, 13
    See also Memorization mapping
Information technology (IT), 133,
    137–139
Initial calls, 134, 136. *See also* Phone calls
Integration, seamless, 122
Internet hardware manufacturing, 85
Interview mapping, 230, 243
Irani, Kaizad, 218–220

Jablokow, Andrei, 133–139
Jobs. *See* Employment
Journal maps, 230, 232

Kaplan, Robert, 208
Kelner, Jared, 85–86, 88–89
Key words:
    branches and, 41
    identifying, 50–51
        benefits of, 51–52
        notes and, 52–53
        obstacles and, 63–67
Koh, Robert, 205
Kumar, M., 139

L.L. Bean, xiv, 2
Lacombe, Don, 236–237
Landmark forum, 205–208
Landscape orientation, 40
    branches and, 54
Leadership, 100
    coaching, introduction to, 113–118
    development programs, 203–204
Leadership Coaching: A Practical Guide, 113
The Leadership Group, 141
The Learning Consortium (TLC), xii–xiii,
    xviii, 24, 92, 131
Learning event, software and, 131–133
Length, branches and, 41, 42
Lim, Choon Boo, 205

INDEX

Linear thinking:
  as a barrier to creativity, 26
  ineffectiveness of, 1
  overcoming, 12
Lines, 22
  branches and, 41, 42
    empty, 43
  connections, 68, 70–73
  laws and, 37
Lists, laws of idea mapping and, 37
Llull, Ramon, 21–23
Logic:
  branches and, 41
  laws of idea mapping and, 37

MacKenzie, Gordon, 200, 201
Macomb Intermediate School District,
    xiv, 2
Maggard, Karen, 100–101
Management training, 24
Mapping, history of, 21–23. *See also* Idea
    mapping
MARC Advertising, xiv, 2
Markers:
  branches and, 41
  central image and, 37, 40
  obstacles and, 73–74
Marketing strategies, 102–104
  blooming and flowing, 32
Maynard, Sharon, 178
Mayo Clinic, xiv, 2, 208, 211
Medieval times, mapping and, 22
Meetings:
  blooming and flowing, 32
  branches and, examples of, 86, 88
Memories, 238
Memorization mapping, 231, 244
Memory Power, 126
Messages, lack of organization and, 46–47
Microsoft PowerPoint, 124, 125, 133
Microsoft Project, 235
Microsoft Word, 124, 133
Middle Tennessee State University, xiv, 2
MindeXtension, 113
Mindjet software, 123
  MindManager Pro 6, 122, 123, 124

project planning and, 235
rule breaking and, 197, 203
team mapping process and, 187
Mind mapping, 7, 24
  as the foundation of idea mapping,
    20–21
Mind Matters, results of workshop, 24–25
Mission, 95–100
  mapping, 230, 233
Moore, Terry, 128–131
Motivation, 15

Nast, Jamie, 109
NastGroup, Inc., xii
Ngee Ann Polytechnic, 205
North, Vanda, 24, 92–95, 105, 131–133,
    176
Note taking, 8, 15, 230, 242
  group meetings and, 230, 243
  organization and, lack of, 46–47
  overcoming, 12
  See also Baseline notes
Numbers, laws of idea mapping and, 37

Obstacles, eliminating, 62, 81. *See also*
    specific type
The One to One Future, 169
One to one maps, 168, 169
Operation Smile, xiv, 2
Orbiting the Giant Hairball, 199–202
Order, branches and, 42
Organization, 15. *See also* Landscape
    orientation; Portrait orientation;
    Upside down, writing
Outlines:
  branches and, 42
  key words and, 63

Paper, running out of, 77–78
Parkland College, 218
Parties, 230, 232
Passions, 238. *See also* Hobbies
Patience, 151–152
Pearson Education Australia, 113
Pencils, colored:
  branches and, 41

Index

central image and, 37, 40
See also Color
Pennsylvania College of Optometry
(PCO), xiv, 2, 152
People mapping, 230, 237–238
Pepper, Don, 169
Perfection, drafting and, 75–77
Personal Excellence, xiii
Personal planning maps, 230, 232
Personality types, 174–175, 238
Phone calls, 51, 230, 239. *See also* Cold
calls; Initial calls
Planning, 15
Portrait orientation, 40
Power browse, 176
Presentation mapping, 15, 205–208,
224–225, 227
benefits of, 225–226
blooming and flowing, 32
delivering and, 230, 236–237
introduction, 165, 166
preparing, 25, 230, 236–237
software and, 125
Primal Leadership, 100
Prioritization, 189–190
Problem solving maps, 230, 235
blooming and flowing, 32
creativity and, 2
Process description, 230, 239–240
Productivity, increased, 2
Project management, 124, 139, 230, 235
creativity and, 2
current trends in job demands, 11
Purdue University, 3
Purpose:
branches and, 42
note taking and, 13
defining purpose, 14
determining and achieving, 13–14

Quotes, key words and, 66

Real-time mapping, 79, 203, 205, 230,
243, 252–254
definition of, 248–249
keys to success, 249–252

Recall:
improving, 2
key words and, 52
Relocation, 92–95
Results, note taking and, 13
Review process, 192
Revisions, software and, 123–124
Rogers, Martha, 169
Rule breaking, 196–211

Sales cycle, 133–139
Salesforce.com, 124–125
Saline Leadership Institute, xiv, 2
Schultz, Beth, 152–161
Seiner, Liza, 89–92
September 11, 2001, 218
Sequential order, 26, 33
laws of idea mapping and, 37
Seven Habits of Highly Effective People, xiii, 95
workshops, 7–9
Shaw, Michael, 208–218
Showler, Debbie, 163–171
Simulator project, 139–140
Skill development, 150–152, 175
Software:
benefits of using, 123–125
concerns, 125–127
criteria, 122–123
See also specific type
Software Spectrum, xiv, 2
Space, as an obstacle, 77–78
Status report mapping, 230, 241
Stokes, Gregg, 105, 109
Strategic marketing, 128–131
Structure, radiant, 42
Studying, 15
Supplies, 37, 40–41. *See also specific type*
Symbols:
branches and, 41
determining categories and, 54

Tables, key words and, 66
Talents, 238
Team mapping method, 100, 182,
193–194, 230, 242
benefits, 192

INDEX

consolidation, 187–189
individual maps, 184–186
prioritization, 189–190
review and update, 192
suggestions, 186–187
taking action, 190–191
topic definition, 183–184
Telephone. *See* Phone calls
Theme:
central image and, 37
key words and, 53
Thickness, branches and, 42
Thought organization, 8, 13, 25–27, 231, 245
barriers to, 26
method of, 26
Time management, 6–7
Time saving, 2
current trends in job demands, 11
software concerns and, 126–127
To-do lists, 43–44, 166, 167, 169, 230, 231
Tong, Gan F., 113, 114
Topic:
central image and, 37
defining the, 183–184
Torpey, Michael, 197–199
Toxicology, 153
Trained brain, 14
Training:
examples of branches and, 86, 88
software and, 131–133

Travel, examples of branches and, 86, 88–89
"Tree of Knowledge," 21, 22
"The Tree of the Philosophy of Love," 22, 23

U.S. Army Ammunition Management, xiv, 2
Unblocking, branches and, 42–43
University of Pittsburgh Institute For Entrepreneurial Excellence, xiv, 2
Untrained brain, 14
Updating, 192
Upside down, writing, 68, 69, 70
Use Your Perfect Memory, 78

Vision, 95–97
corporate, 169–171
getting started, 97–100
mapping, 230, 233
VoiceAmerica.com, xiii

The Wall Street Journal, 123
Webbing, 176
Website design mapping, 231, 244
Wilkins, Pete, 104, 141, 142
Willow Run High School, xiv, 2, 177–178
Words, laws of idea mapping and, 37
World Trade Center Memorial Park, 218–220

The Youthful Tooth Company, 102–104

About the CD-ROM

We hope you have enjoyed *Idea Mapping*. To help you explore your interest in this topic, this CD-ROM contains introductory resources for Mindjet® MindManager®Pro 6, including:

- A 21-day trial version of MindManager Pro 6
- A QuickStart Guide to introduce you to MindManager Pro 6 basics
- An animated Quick Tour of MindManager
- Cases Studies describing how companies and people use MindManager Pro 6 to improve their work processes
- Use Cases explaining how you can use MindManager Pro 6 in your work

Contents of This Readme

Here is a list of the contents of this Readme:

- MindManager Content Overview
- System requirements for the contents of this CD
- How to install MindManager Pro 6
- How to purchase MindManager Pro 6
- How to contact Mindjet

MindManager Content Overview

MindManager Pro 6

- Trial Version of MindManager Pro 6
- Mindjet MindManager QuickStart Guide.pdf

MindManager Flash demonstrations

(Flash Player and Internet Browser Required)

- Mindjet MindManager 6 Quick Tour

MindManager Use Cases

(Adobe Reader Required)

- Aggregate and Manage Content
- Brainstorm and Capture Ideas
- Draft and Write Presentations, Speeches, and Reports
- Conduct a SWOT analysis
- Enhance Strategic Thinking and Planning
- Enhance Learning

265

- Improve Teaching Quality
- Collaborate with Teams

MindManager Case Studies
(Adobe Reader Required)

- **Allied Telesyn:** *Meeting Management and Process Improvement*
  In a down economy, Allied Telesyn used MindManager to more than triple its profitability, while improving its employees' ability to think strategically and work efficiently. The Chief Operating Officer credits the company's success to the efficient collaboration and concise documentation enabled by MindManager.
- **Professor Jerry Kang, UCLA:** *Information Management, Teaching, and Writing*
  A law professor uses MindManager to increase his students' learning and satisfaction, and to organize his research and writing. Class lectures are prepared more efficiently and are presented in a clearer and more compelling form: a MindManager map.
- **Maryland Applied Information Technology Initiative (MAITI):** *Complex IT Information Management*
  An education executive uses MindManager to capture, re-access and communicate complex information on emerging high technology issues
- **MatrixDM:** *Business Planning*
  MatrixDM Marketing and Consulting used MindManager to plan and launch its business, and then to create iterative strategic plans that enable it to respond quickly to changing market conditions.
- **SRK Consulting:** *Process Improvement*
  A global engineering consulting firm leverages the intellectual capital of 500 employees on 5 continents . . . runs faster, more effective meetings, resulting in wins of new and incremental client business.
- **IBC:** *Process Improvement*
  The president of this $2 Billion industrial & bearing supply group uses MindManager for Tablet PC to share knowledge on key accounts, maintain strategic vision, and make key decisions quickly.
- **Genencor International, Inc:** *Biotech Information Management and Project Planning*
  The president of a biotech company uses MindManager to create a virtual consortium of six universities, two biotech companies and a government research institute. Its goal: To develop new medical technologies that will improve the response to biochemical weapons of mass destruction and other threats to public health.

System Requirements

You will need the following software to access these files:

- Mindjet MindManager 6
- Macromedia Flash Player
- Adobe Reader

A trial version of MindManager is on this CD. The Flash Player and Adobe Reader are free and available from the web.

You will also need an Internet browser for the Flash Player. Check the Flash Player system requirements on the web.

Installing MindManager Pro 6

The MindManager Pro 6 installer is located on this CD.

To install MindManager Pro 6:

1. Double-click on its icon to launch the installer.
2. Enter the following information when prompted by the installer:
    * Select your country.
    * Accept the license agreement.
    * Enter your user name, organization, and license key. (optional)
    * Select the setup type. (We recommend a complete setup)
    * Choose your shortcuts.
3. Click Install.
4. At the prompt, click **Finish** to complete the installation.

Congratulations! You have now installed MindManager Pro 6.

Purchasing MindManager Pro 6

Each time you launch a trial version of MindManager, you see a prompt asking you to:

* Buy the product
* Enter the license key
* Continue

If you are ready to purchase the product, click **Buy.** Your Internet browser will open to the Mindjet Purchase Options page. Follow the instructions on that page to complete your purchase.

Contacting Mindjet

Thank you for your interest in Mindjet and Mindjet MindManager Pro 6. You can contact Mindjet from this URL: http://www.mindjet.com/us/company/about_mindjet/contact_us/index.php?s=6

This web page has a complete list of links for contacting sales, media relations, or the web master.

For information about the CD-ROM, see the About the CD-ROM section on pages 265–267.